Books by Caskie Stinnett

WILL NOT RUN FEBRUARY 22ND

OUT OF THE RED

BACK TO ABNORMAL

GRAND AND PRIVATE PLEASURES

Grand and
Private Pleasures

Grand and Private Pleasures

by CASKIE STINNETT

An Atlantic Monthly Press Book

LITTLE, BROWN AND COMPANY · BOSTON · TORONTO

COPYRIGHT © 1966, 1967, 1972, 1973, 1974, 1975, 1976, 1977
BY CASKIE STINNETT

LIBRARY OF CONGRESS CATALOGING IN PUBLICATION DATA

Stinnett, Caskie.
    Grand and private pleasures.

    "An Atlantic Monthly Press book."
    1. Voyages and travels—1951-   I. Title.
G464.S724   910'.4   77-22416
ISBN 0-316-81629-9

FIRST EDITION
T11/77

Portions of this book have appeared in *The Atlantic Monthly,*
Travel and Leisure, Holiday, and *The Holiday Inn Companion.*

ATLANTIC–LITTLE, BROWN BOOKS
ARE PUBLISHED BY
LITTLE, BROWN AND COMPANY
IN ASSOCIATION WITH
THE ATLANTIC MONTHLY PRESS

Published simultaneously in Canada
by Little, Brown & Company (Canada) Limited

PRINTED IN THE UNITED STATES OF AMERICA

For Lillian Hellman

Preface

I HAVE traveled widely in my lifetime, having been struck by the virus at an early age and having, as yet, developed no antibodies to harden my resistance or immunity. I have no idea how *much* I have traveled, and I have not the slightest intention of ever trying to total it up in miles, an exercise that seems irresistible to many travelers who are fond of saying their transatlantic crossings would carry them halfway to the moon or otherwise equating their earthly ramblings with some galactic measure. E. B. White, a man not the least impressed with meaningless figures, once wrote that "the commuter dies with tremendous mileage to his credit, but he is no rover." I like to think of myself as a rover, and I am bringing up the matter of my own travel only to buttress my otherwise shaky qualifications as an authority in the matter. I am writing these lines in mid-Manhattan, but a cursory inventory of the objects closest at hand is surprising even to me now that I see them catalogued. The slacks I am wearing I bought in Jamaica, and my undershorts were made in Communist China but were purchased in Hong Kong. My shoes came from a small and forgotten bootery on New Bond Street in London. My wristwatch was bought in Sion, a very small city in Switzerland; the strap came from a concourse shop beneath Rockefeller Plaza — the Swiss make good watches but poor straps. My most recent haircut I got a week ago in Rio de Janeiro, and I am squeezing the end of a seemingly endless ribbon of toothpaste from a tube I bought in Taipei. It is very poor and I will be pleased when it is gone. My present suitcase I bought on a Sunday morning in Nadi, which is in Fiji, where this suitcase's predecessor fell suddenly apart. My left forearm aches from a cholera booster, which I got in preparation for a trip to Bombay.

My friend Lillian Hellman, who thinks travel is an invention of the devil, has said it is "inhuman" that I should travel as I do and not disintegrate from the ordeal. She marvels that one could return from Australia one day and depart for Africa the next, seemingly in good health and spirits. This would indeed be something to marvel at if one did it constantly, because long periods of travel under the best of circumstances can be exhausting; what I have never been able to make my friend understand is that there is an art to travel, a means of getting the most out of a trip with a minimum of effort. She doesn't understand this because she approaches travel with dread and foreboding. A traveler whose circuits are thus overloaded to begin with, hasn't a chance.

Travel makes up for its discomforts by supplying passengers with megadoses of a supplementary vitamin, the need for which in human nutrition may not yet have been established but whose presence in a trip has a bracing effect upon an individual. This is the exhilarating sense of adventure which, when all is said and done, is what travel is all about. Travel stripped of adventure is almost inevitably an exercise imbedded in monotony; without it the traveler moves through strange lands untouched and touching nothing. I have been pulled out of quicksand in an Amazon jungle, I have spent the best part of a winter's day locked up in Elsinore Castle, and I once swam in the Coral Sea in an area that I was told — later — was the greatest breeding place in the world for sharks, but these are not necessarily the adventures that travelers need experience. Perhaps what I want to say is that one should use travel as a means of living out fantasies, of making the bright dream materialize. Take the Orient Express from Munich to Vienna, despite the fact that flying is quicker. Spend a night in an Irish castle, despite the fact that the bathroom is a long way away. See for yourself how a family of lions behave on the high plateaus of Kenya or how a family of Stone Age mudmen behave in the highlands of New Guinea. Both have been around a long time but they show every sign of an early departure.

Travel is a personal thing, like raising a family, and to reduce it to a science, as the tour operators have done, is to make it meaningless. It is too delicate to be homogenized, sterilized, and rendered so predictable that one may as well remain in one's living room. The notion of travel is based upon a desire to escape, at least temporarily, from the familiar, the known, the totally secure. Travel demands more determination than courage; a determination to participate and not to play the role of an observer. The airlines have come to refer to travelers as "seats" and hotels refer to them as "beds"; this offends me but it shows how far down the road to mass manipulation we have drifted.

Because travel is such a personal experience, I suspect you may encounter me in the chapters of this book more frequently than you care to. I'm genuinely apologetic about this, but I don't know any other way to do it. I find I write with great elation about the places that appeal to me, and I'm dispirited in dealing with those that don't, and it appears that I am not able to keep these feelings from spilling over the tiny levee of self-discipline that I have managed to erect. My notion of a fine subject to write about is an early morning walk down a country lane in Yorkshire in the late fall; a mist hangs over the brook that meanders through the meadow, the air is crisp, and there's a hint of wood smoke coming from some undisclosed source. Or how it feels to sit at dusk with a cup of hot chocolate in the Piazza della Signoria in Florence and allow oneself to become bewitched by the meddlesome spirit of Fra Savonarola, who was put to death for his mischief in that same square. Or walk on a winter's day along the Penobscot coast of Maine, with snow stacked in the sky, and to breathe deeply of salt air sweetened by balsam. All of these subjects deal with mood rather than place, with shadow rather than substance. It's my contention that travel is most rewarding when it is felt, that observation alone doesn't give you your money's worth. I shall never forget one fine spring day in Sicily when I rounded a curve approaching Agrigento and for the first time in my life I came — dramatically and abruptly — upon the grandeur of Greece. On a grassy hill above me stood the ruins of a Greek temple, its thirty-six Doric columns rising with enormous dignity to the sky. The effect was almost that of a blow. This was a rare combination of seeing and feeling, a sensual confluence that the traveler often yearns for but seldom experiences.

While I'm clearing the air, perhaps it would be fair if I set forth my likes and dislikes, so that readers may take a look, as they might at a smorgasbord table, to see if there is anything there they would care to sample. All seasons can be delightful, but I prefer spring. The Italian word *prima-vera* says it. Scotland, I'm convinced, is the most beautiful country in the world, although the island of Java is almost as magnificent but in a totally different way. There is a sweet-sadness in the heart of Italy that captivates me, and I believe that London is the last stronghold of the male in the Western world. Washington is a pretty city but a dull capital, and New York is gritty and tense. I like riding on a train in the rain, eating breakfast outdoors, reading a news-paper in a park, especially the park in Vancouver that doesn't permit transistor radios. I'm uneasy about unan-nounced delays in plane departures, beach hotels that do their best to discourage swimming, mountain cable cars, the atmosphere of gambling casinos, and the operetta royalty of some of Europe's smaller nations. I can't guarantee that these prejudices won't surface in this book, so it's good that you know about them at the outset and can make other plans.

What more than anything do I want to say about the pleasure of travel? Do things that you have dreamed of but wouldn't do at home. Be adventurous, be a little bit reck-less, *participate*. Remember, you are seeing people as they do not see themselves; permit them to see you the same way. Spend a night in the little hillside village that captured your imagination from the train window. Get off at the next station, get a taxi, and go back there. You will never regret it, even though the bed may be lumpy, the street steep, and the food poor. It will have become your town and you will henceforth be fiercely possessive of it.

Once, long ago, I occupied an apartment in Portofino for a brief period. Portofino, if there is anyone left who hasn't been there, is a cluster of pastel-colored buildings around a very small harbor in northern Italy. Olive groves rise steeply behind the harbor, and aside from the swarm of summer visitors nothing much ever happens in the village.. But in the summer and early autumn the days are golden, with lizards scuttling in the sunlight, and the nights are dim and strange with that cool stagnancy that seems to pervade all Mediterranean towns. It was a quiet and uneventful period, but I recall it with immense pleasure. Do you see what I mean?

I ask you to eat lunch in a laborers' tavern or buy a bag of fruit in the village market and munch it on the bluff overlooking the river. Sit over a cup of tea on a rainy day in the railroad station and watch the others with their cakes and beer, and enjoy the uproar, the humidity, the heat, the crowd. Or order a glass of wine in a cheap open-air café under the chestnut trees, and watch the old men reading their papers, or take silent sides in the petanque match, or just sit quietly and watch the motorbikes roar by. Drive outside the city and walk among the fiery autumn trees, especially early in the morning when the cool mist still hangs over everything, and drink pastis, if you are in France, or ouzo, if you are in Greece, or grappa, if you are in Italy. Eat the cassoulet of the workers, or the moussaka, or the salami. Choose the rocky paths and lanes, despite the dust and loose stones, because they will lead you to where you can see geese on the march, and hear insects buzzing, and the rumble of traffic gives way to the carpenter's hammer and the idle chatter of ducks as they waddle off to some creek or waterhole. I believe in walking; if you see something that interests you it is possible to stop on a dime and investigate the object of your interest closely and in a way that is impossible while motoring. Often at night in a strange city I will stand and stare until I get the place in my mind. "I am in Copenhagen," I will say to myself over and over until my mind accepts it. Know where you are if you later want to know where you have been.

— Caskie Stinnett

Contents

[xvii]

Grand and
Private Pleasures

1

The Green Hell of Leticia

Less than one hundred yards from where I am sitting on the porch of a cottage in Leticia — a steaming little jungle town situated on the bank of the Amazon River at a point where Colombia, Brazil and Peru come together — lies the world's greatest river, a muddy, sullen, fast-flowing body of water pushing its way to the Atlantic Ocean two thousand miles away. Yesterday I was warned by a jungle guide against the river's whirlpools; once caught in one, he said, a man could surface twenty minutes later a mile downstream. Moreover, the river is alive with piranha, an evil, ferocious little fish that, in schools, can reduce a man to a skeleton in less than a minute. There are stinger-rays, leeches, freshwater sharks and God knows what other horrors lurking in those silt-laden currents and backwaters, and nobody who knows anything about the river would dream of immersing even a hand in it. A few days ago in a boat, I undertook to baste myself under the hot equatorial sun and I scooped up a bucket of river water to pour over my body. There were two piranhas in the bucket. The only exception to this hostile river life is the existence in the Amazon — and nowhere else — of a species of pink dolphin, the sight of

[3]

which is supposed to bring the viewer good luck. Late in an afternoon as I was returning in a small boat from the Peruvian side of the river, I saw one: a dramatic flash of pink arching above the muddy water. A few minutes later the motor conked out and the boatman and I drifted five miles into Brazil before it started up again, so I'm skeptical about the dolphin's gift of good luck. Maybe without the dolphin it wouldn't have started at all.

The Amazon Basin is the world's biggest water system, and there is nothing much that it can be compared to. Everything about it is staggering and anything one writes about it is likely to be understatement. It drains some 2,800,000 square miles of what has come to be known as the Green Hell, a dense and deadly jungle spread out over five South American countries. So much oxygen is released from the vegetation that it is referred to by scientists as the Lungs of the World and once it is tamed and defoliated — if that ever happens — the envelope of atmosphere surrounding the planet will probably no longer support life. It is estimated that the Amazon River pours nearly seven million cubic feet of water *per second* into the Atlantic Ocean, and the salinity of the sea is altered by this massive discharge of fresh water as far as two hundred miles from the mouth of the river. The Amazon contains one-fifth of the world's fresh water supply. At its widest point it is forty miles from bank to bank, but at Leticia it is perhaps two miles wide, which accounts for the brisk currents that sweep through the river here. One sees the Peruvian bank easily enough, but I doubt that one could make out a man standing there. Oceangoing vessels can sail past Leticia all the way to Iquitos, a Peruvian town twenty-three hundred miles from the river's mouth at Belém, Brazil, although why anyone would want to go so far for so little I can't imagine. Still, compared to Leticia, Iquitos must seem like Paris. Leticia is a handful of houses, a tiny airport, a few stores, a couple of small hotels, and some dusty or muddy streets — depending upon the season — sweltering under the unrelenting sun of the equator, which lies only 120 miles to the north. The jungle threatens to engulf it, and if at any moment the entire village disappeared I wouldn't be in the least surprised. It's a tenuous foothold.

Flying into Leticia from Bogotá, one gets the impression the pilot must be lost because there is no break in the jungle as far as one can see. Then suddenly the river comes into view; then the cluster of buildings that is Leticia; and finally a tiny airstrip materializes. The runway is an engineering miracle, built by Colombian labor in nine months despite the fact that there was not a single stone within a radius of two hundred miles. Sand and gravel were dredged up from the river, and a runway was built that will hold up under fairly large planes. From the airport terminal I telephoned Mike Tsalikis, a wild animal hunter I had been instructed to look up, and he told me to wait there until he could send a jeep for me. The jeep arrived promptly and took me to the Hotel Parador Ticuna, a group of small cottages, owned by Tsalikis and his brother George, not far from the river. The town's other hotel is called the Anaconda. While the name was intriguing, I figured I would be better off at a place where I had a contact with someone.

It's hot here. The lights flicker when the generator falters, and the bottle of beer I just took from the refrigerator in my room was cool but far from cold. Just outside my door is a small swimming pool, a startling sight in a village like Leticia, and while the water stays at body temperature it is at least wet. During the past few nights I have

[5]

slipped naked in the pool a half-dozen times, and it helps some, especially when I emerge and lie wet in a hammock until I doze off.

Leticia is called a port but there is no port here in the usual sense of the word. A few river steamers and some Colombian gunboats tie up along the bank overnight, but if any passengers go ashore they don't stay long. What there is to see in the village can be seen quickly. The Amazon has a high embankment at Leticia, which protects the village against floods — a constant peril in these vast flatlands — and there's nothing much along the embankment except a few shacks and Eduardo's Bar. I stopped in the bar a few days ago and was surprised to find it occupied, at the moment, only by Eduardo and half a dozen chickens who apparently considered it home. It was difficult to estimate when it had been last swept out; perhaps never. I had a warm beer and a cordial smile from the proprietor, and left. Beer was one of two drinks dispensed by Eduardo, the other being Colombiana, a very sweet soft drink possessing no taste whatever. I customarily washed down my meals with Colombiana because it is bottled in Bogotá and I reasoned it was safer than the local water.

Yesterday I arose early, dressed, and walked down to the river to have a look at the market, which I had been told disappeared completely by seven-thirty. It was spread out on the embankment in wild disorder, offering an assortment of fruit, strange vegetables, and fish of all kinds but mostly the giant catfish that lurk in the murky channels and that often grow to be monsters of six hundred pounds or more. Since refrigeration is rare in Leticia, everything has to be fresh and most of the fish had just been brought from the river and were being disemboweled on the spot. Flies clung to fish and entrails alike; the embankment was

[6]

blanketed in blood and offal. I saw a villager study a small pile of roots, select two, and drop a coin into the hand of an Indian who had brought them from somewhere in the jungle. Money is money everywhere. She moved on to watch the work of an elderly black man who was carving up a fish; it wasn't a catfish but more like a pirarucu, a fighting fish that moves through the water like a bullet. She indicated the cut she wanted, marking the fish with her finger, and accepted the dripping piece of meat wrapped crudely in a leaf. Dugout canoes loaded with fish and fruit were still pulling up to the mudbank when I decided I had seen enough, and started to walk up the single street that led from the river. On the edge of the crowd, a seated woman was selling some kind of fried pastry. The pieces were arranged on a clean cloth as she took them from the fire. Business was slow.

Another day I am taken across the river in search of *Victoria regia* on the Peruvian side. *Victoria regia* is the massive water lily whose circular leaf is so broad it can support the weight of a small child. My boatman, who spoke no English, pulled the boat up on the mudbank and motioned for me to follow him. We moved down the river for several hundred yards, and then started inland. The boatman moved with the confidence of a man who knew where he was going. We crossed a large sandbar that had been left by a flood, then pushed up a steep incline covered with undergrowth. There are some extremely poisonous snakes in the Amazon, including both the bushmaster and the fer-de-lance, and I was uncomfortable walking where I could not see, but the boatman seemed unconcerned. We came to a small lake, muddy like the river, that had become landlocked by receding floodwater. There were no *Victoria regiae*, and the boatman looked baffled. He picked up a

[7]

stick and threw it in the water. The impact of the stick upon the surface of the lake set off a surge of underwater motion that was startling. "Muchos piranha," the boatman said, grinning. I gathered that as the water evaporated under the hot sun and the food supply diminished, the imprisoned piranha would strike at anything that moved, even a stick.

I eat my meals in a small dining room where all of the guests of the Parador Ticuna come together, but since there are only a few of us — some Avianca stewardesses were here a few nights ago, but that was unusual — we occupy only one table and conversation is stilted and dull. Things improve when George Tsalikis is present; he is an affable, intelligent man who, like his brother, came to the Amazon jungle from Tarpon Springs, Florida, in search of an interesting way of life and found it. A few evenings ago, George offered to make me a Pisco sour, an explosive drink made from a Peruvian liquor that possesses much of the quality of tequila. I don't know what else the drink contained, other than a generous portion of Pisco and an egg white, but it was both powerful and refreshing. The menu runs heavily to fish since most meat would have to be flown in frozen from Bogotá. A typical dinner would consist of fried catfish, rice, noodles, meatballs, salad and canned figs. Not a meal, as Samuel Johnson would say, to invite a man to, but certainly adequate.

A few evenings ago I organized a small group to dine out at the local *charruscaria*, a sort of barbecue place a few doors down the street from the Anaconda Hotel. We ate outside, the group consisting of George and a friend, a chap from the Colombia tourist office who had come down on the plane from Bogotá with me, and a jungle guide with his girlfriend from San Francisco. The guide, whose name was John, had worked hard, saved a bit of money, and was preparing to go back to the United States to enter college. His girlfriend, a tall and pretty blonde with delicate features, seemed out of place in Leticia, but said she had found the place fascinating and frequently went into the jungle with John. After a few beers, we looked to George to order dinner for us all. He ordered in Spanish, a language I have no grasp of, and I didn't ask him to explain what we were getting. Fortunately the meat was charred and unrecognizable, and I was on the whole pleased not to know what it was.

A few years ago Colombia enacted some very stringent conservation laws that seriously curtailed Mike Tsalikis's operations in capturing and exporting wild animals, most of which went to zoos around the world. A few, mostly snakes and sloths, remain in pens in a building beside the Parador Ticuna. Neither Mike nor George knows at this time what he will do with these captives, the most likely course of action being to turn them loose again in the jungle. One day when I was wandering idly through the building, I came upon George trying to get a sloth back in its cage with a long pole.

The sloth responded to the jabbing and backed into the cage and George closed the door. "How would you like to hold a seventeen-foot boa constrictor?" George asked me.

I hesitated. "What's the danger?" I asked. "What would it do?"

"Nothing," George replied, "if you held its mouth tightly shut. It has a mean bite but it's not poisonous. Take a look at it." He led me to the other end of the building, where there was a pen containing fifteen or twenty snakes of all colors and sizes. One, an immense thing as thick as my thigh, was curled up in a tight ball, and George began to poke at it with his stick. "Wake up," George said. "We have a visitor." The snake made no effort to uncoil, so George went in the pen and dragged it out, closing the door behind him. The snake slumped lazily on the floor. "Hold its mouth shut with both hands," he said, "like this." He wrapped both hands tightly around the snake's mouth. The snake's eyes were yellow and they regarded George impassively. I did as I was told, while George uncoiled the snake and placed it around my shoulders. I almost buckled at the knees from the weight. Although the snake was sluggish and showed not the slightest interest in me, I could feel the power of its muscles as its weight shifted and its tail began to encircle my waist. "How does it feel?" asked George. "Heavy," I replied, "and not terribly friendly. Take it back." I continued to hold the snake's mouth while George lifted it from me, and together we carried it back to the pen. George opened the door, and we placed the boa constrictor on the floor. I released its mouth and stepped back quickly; the snake began to coil itself slowly into a ball. "That's a mean thing to meet in the jungle," George said. "It anchors one end with its teeth, while its tail searches around for something to hold to. Then it starts to constrict. There's not much that can break that hold once both ends are anchored."

It is, I suppose, impractical to weave any sort of political, cultural and economic fabric across an area as sprawling as the Amazon Basin and the Mato Grosso jungle, especially since there are so many Indian tribes who care nothing about national governments and who are often even unaware of their existence. Consequently, travel between Peru, Colombia, and Brazil in this area is informal and unhindered; there are no border guards or customs agents, and the currency of all three countries is accepted without question among the jungle people. I crossed borders two or three times a day and was often unaware of it. This wasn't always the case. Leticia was Peruvian until 1922, when that country ceded the village and surrounding area to Colombia, and border disputes were frequent and unpleasant. In 1932, a particularly hostile dispute escalated into an all-out war between the two countries and it was settled only after intervention by the League of Nations.

In the late afternoon of the next to the last day of my visit to Leticia, I was having a drink under the thatched-roof shelter that served as a bar, when John, the guide, came up and took a seat at my table. I offered him a drink and he chose a beer. It was served in the bottle with no accompanying glass; frontier villages don't put much stock in empty flourishes. "I'm going into the jungle tomorrow looking for a Yagua village that I've heard about," he said. "Would you care to come with me? It may be a tough hike." I considered it a moment then promptly accepted. I wanted to see the jungle before I left. John took a long pull from the bottle and sat it down on the table. It wouldn't be easy, he told me, and we might be gone all day. Be prepared for anything. Wear a shirt with long sleeves and trousers. No shorts. Put something on my head, anything. Don't take anything unnecessary, and if it is raining the trip is off. I nodded assent. "I'd like to start early," he said, draining the bottle and getting to his feet. "Six, anyway. We'll go upriver in a boat about twenty miles and start out from there. Okay?" I said okay.

John was waiting at the river when I arrived there the next morning. It was ten minutes to six. He was wearing boots and he had a machete in a scabbard hanging from his belt. He looked businesslike. "We're not taking any lunch," he announced. "If we're not back by lunchtime, you can live on some of that fat around your waist." I laughed and got in the boat. It was a long, narrow craft with a strange-looking motor mounted on the stern. "Sit up front," John said, "and take this." He passed me a six-pack of beer, which I stowed under my seat. John pushed off with a long pole, which he carefully placed on the floor of the boat. He made an adjustment on the motor, and yanked a cord. It started easily, and we began to move upstream. John steered close to the bank. "There's less current here," he explained. "Out there in the middle we'd only go half this fast. Coming back we'll be out there looking for currents."

We rode in silence. John looked ahead for floating logs or patches of river vine that would foul the propeller. The air was cool and fresh, and I watched the bank for signs of life. From time to time we would pass a shack, built on the highest piece of land possible, with two or three naked children playing around the edge of the water, but the shacks grew farther and farther apart as we traveled upstream and they finally disappeared entirely. Once I saw what appeared to be a dog swimming, and I pointed it out to John. "Let's take the dog to the shore," I said. John turned the boat in the direction of the dog. "If it's a dog," he said, "you can bet that it's already dead." When we got closer I could see that he was right. The dog was bloated in death, and it had appeared to be swimming because it was being pulled apart by piranha. John headed the boat back toward the bank and we continued on upstream.

It was nearly eight o'clock and the sun was getting hot when he pulled up to a sandbar and cut the motor. "This is as good a place as any to tie up," he said. We both got out, and John dragged the boat up on the sand. It felt good to stretch my legs. "We'll have a beer and then get going," he said, reaching under my seat for the six-pack. While we drank the beer, John studied me carefully. "Take off your wristwatch," he said, "and take out your wallet and remove that glass fish on the string around your neck, and get rid of anything that you absolutely don't need. Strip down to essentials." I asked if I could carry a camera, and he said that I could. "I'll probably have to bring it out," he said, "but go ahead and take it."

I took my valuables and held them out to him, and he dropped them casually in a small compartment under his seat where he kept a few tools. "If anybody comes around the boat they will find your things," he said, "but river people aren't inclined to snoop around." I slung my camera around my neck. "Does anybody know where we are?" I asked. "I mean, if we should have trouble in the jungle." John laughed. "Mike and George know what we're doing," he said. "The minute they saw the boat on the sandbar, they'd know exactly where to look for us. Let's get moving."

We climbed up the embankment, John carrying the long pole he had taken from the floor of the boat. At the last minute he had put a small canvas bag around his neck, and let it hang loosely under one arm. I don't know what the bag contained but I saw him force-feed two bottles of beer into it. At the top of the embankment, the jungle began. It was like going through a door.

A jungle is a sweltering, wet, muddy wilderness that seems to have no beginning and no end. There are vines everywhere; I was surprised at their toughness and the way they grasp an invader. Where the vegetation is less dense one can see the sky, but more often the foliage blankets everything. Progress is painfully slow. John moved well ahead of me, swinging the machete with measured strokes;

there was no overkill, no wasted exertion. I slipped awk-wardly in the mud, and twice fell to the ground, but slowly I learned to steady myself by clinging to vines. "If you start to fall," John shouted to me from ahead, "don't fight it. The mud won't hurt you. It's when you fight it that you sprain something."

At the end of the first half-hour, John had gotten so far ahead of me that he stopped and waited for me to catch up with him. He had a grin on his face. "You're a real mess," he said, looking at my clothes. My shirt was drenched with sweat, and I was covered with mud. I looked inquiringly at the canvas bag, thinking of the beer it contained, and John read my thoughts. "Forget about the beer," he said firmly. "That's to drink on our way out." We started up again, John hacking away at the vines. I fell behind perhaps ten yards or so, and made an effort to maintain the pace. We moved along surprisingly fast, but gradually John forged ahead of me until I could hardly hear him swinging the machete. I was startled to come upon him suddenly. We had come to a low point, and the mud had given way to water. There were fallen trees and rotten logs everywhere. "If you took my pole to steady yourself," he asked, "do you think you could walk on those logs? I'm not sure what's in the water, probably nothing, but I'd rather have you on the logs. It seems to get higher again pretty soon so there is not much of this." I took the pole. John stepped on a log, walked to the end of it, then moved to another. It looked easy, but it wasn't, not even with the pole. Several times I slipped off the logs into black water up to the knees, but crawled quickly back. The pole helped immensely, but it tended to get stuck in the mud and pulling it out nearly upset my balance a couple of times. John had already reached a high point and was waiting for me. "I hope we don't run into too much of that," he said. "It slows us down."

He moved on ahead of me. When I caught up with him again he was standing on the edge of a small clearing. There was a trace of anxiety on his face. In front of him was a sea of mud, broken up by small tufts of grass. "This isn't quicksand," he said, "but it's mud and just as bad. There's no bottom to it. I've run into a lot of this. If you can step on the patches of grass, there is good footing but you have to keep moving. If you slip off you're in trouble. I'd be inclined to walk around it but there's no telling how far we would have to go. Want to try it or go back?" I wanted very much to go back, but I couldn't bring myself to say it. "Let's try it," I said.

John thought for a moment. "All right," he said, "we'll try it. Now listen to me because this isn't a game. First, we stay as close together as we can. Second, if you should slip, and feel a foot going into the mud, don't panic and try to run out. You'll only sink with both feet. Lie down and roll toward me as fast as you can roll. Got it?" I nodded my head. John asked me for my camera, which I removed from around my neck and passed to him. "Let's move as fast as we can," he said, "and I want you to step in my tracks. But don't slow down and don't get too far behind me. These clumps of grass will support us for only a few seconds." There was a moment's pause, and John started forward. Head down, I followed grimly. I gazed only at his feet. As he lifted a foot, I placed mine down in the exact spot a second later. He went up to his ankles in mud with each step and I went even deeper, but we kept moving. It was strangely exciting. Suddenly there was no empty track to step into, I was too close on him. I reached out quickly to him, and stepped in the mud to keep from falling. My right leg went into the mud up to my thigh, and I shouted. Turning quickly, John grasped my hand and jerked me forward. There was an empty track and I found it. We moved forward again. In less than a minute, we had reached a clump of underbrush and firm ground. I sat on the end of a rotten log, trembling violently. There was no bottom to the mud, I could tell that when my leg sank into it. "That was a little scary," John said quietly. "But going back won't be so bad, because you'll know what to do. Just don't crowd me so closely next time."

It was perhaps an hour later that we came upon a cow, grazing in a small clearing. John brightened. "We must be near a village," he said. "The jaguars would get that cow if there weren't people nearby." We were climbing to higher ground now, and the vegetation was less thick. John had put the machete back in the scabbard. In a few minutes we emerged into an open space; there were five thatched-roof huts scattered about the clearing. For the first time I noticed that the sky had turned black, and thunder was rolling through the jungle. An old woman, naked except for a small fragment of red cloth around her waist, was squatting beside a fire, stirring a liquid in a black pot. The liquid was gray and there were fishheads floating in it. It looked awful. John squatted beside her silently, and took the canvas bag from around his neck. Feeling under the bottles of beer, he brought out a handful of caramels. The old woman didn't speak but pointed toward one of the huts. John straightened up and, with me following, walked to the hut. An ancient Indian man, naked and carrying a blowgun, came out. He gazed vacantly at John, who handed him the caramels. The old man felt the candy and smiled. "This is the chief," John said over his shoulder to me, "and he seems to be blind. There is a lot of blindness among these Indians." I looked at the old man's eyes and they were clouded over with cataracts. He led us to his hut, and climbed a short ladder. John and I followed him. The hut, built on stilts, contained only one room. There were three young women sitting on the floor and, like the old woman by the fire, each was wearing only a red piece of cloth around her waist. They had high cheekbones, and no trace of coarseness in their faces. They giggled at us, and eagerly accepted the caramels that John offered. "These are probably the chief's wives," John explained, "but I doubt that he has been able to have children for a long time. The men are probably all out hunting. They only come home at night when it's too dark to hunt. I've been told there are only about one thousand Yaguas left in the entire jungle. They originally came from Peru, and all they do is hunt. They don't grow crops at all, and never have. They hunt with blowguns mostly, although in recent years some of them have gotten shotguns. I once saw a Yagua bring down a bird in flight with a blowgun from five hundred feet away. They are deadly shots."

It started to rain, a violently descending wall of water, but the hut was dry. One of the women went down the ladder quickly, and came back carrying a wet baby in her arms. The baby was completely naked, and didn't seem to mind the water at all. The mother took a piece of caramel out of her mouth and gave it to the baby who swallowed it with relish. John took out more candy and passed it around; it was accepted with more giggles. I asked John if he had ever visited these people before, and he said that he didn't think so but couldn't be sure. He may have seen them at some other camp. "Whenever a child dies," he said, "they burn down the village and move away. They blame the death on the location of the camp. As you might imagine, it causes them to move around a lot."

About sixty miles up the river there was a fairly large Yagua village, John said, and scattered throughout the jungle in the general area of Leticia were a number of Ticuna villages. In general, he thought, the Ticuna were less primitive than the Yagua. "When Mike Tsalikis comes upon a camp and finds a sick child," he said, "he tries to take it into the village for medical attention, but this isn't easy with these people. It's hard to explain to them that the doctors may be able to make the child well again."

The rain showed no sign of slackening, and I asked John what he proposed to do. "There's no sense in trying to wait it out," he said, "because it could stop any time or go on for five or six more hours. I think we should head on back. Besides the rain will make things cooler." He fished a pack of cigarettes out of the canvas bag, and walked over to the corner where the old man was sitting. He held the old man's hand while he put the cigarettes in it. A smile crinkled the old man's face. "He looks ancient," John said to me, "and he's probably about forty-five. Or he may be a hundred. Who knows? I'm sure he doesn't." We crawled down the ladder in the rain. In thirty seconds I was soaked, but John was right. It was cool. We started through the jungle again.

I doubt that I could have picked up our trail, but John found it easily and he seemed happy not to be using the machete. We moved much more swiftly on the return, and we passed the bog without mishap. On the other side of the bog, John stopped to take out the beer. He snapped the tops off both bottles and handed me one. It was warm and the foam ran down the side of the bottle, but it was wet and I drank it gratefully. He threw the two bottles in the mud and we watched as they silently sank out of sight.

Two hours later we were back at the boat. The rain had stopped but the sky was still overcast and it was unbearably hot. I took off my shirt and trousers and waded into the river, where I swam a dozen strokes or so and then turned and walked quickly out. John eyed me critically. "That was a stupid thing to do," he said. I shrugged. "I'm sure it was," I said, "but I feel better." We pushed the boat off the sandbar, and John pointed it toward midstream. An hour and a half later we were having a Colombiana in Eduardo's Bar.

I left Leticia the next day. The Avianca pilot, to whom I had been introduced in the airport, sent word to me that I would be welcome on the flight deck, and I made my way forward. The view from the front of the plane was superb. We were flying up the river, and I was struck again by the vastness of the jungle that seemed to stretch out endlessly on both sides of the Amazon. We were gaining altitude quickly, and I strained to see if I could identify the sandbar where we had beached the boat the day before, but landmarks at that height had begun to blur. All I could make out was a dark green wilderness threaded by an immense brown river.

2

The Best Ham in the World. Period.

VIRGINIA Route 10 meanders southward from Richmond through scrub pine country, paralleling the James River most of the way, and shortly before it is swallowed up in the Chesapeake Bay area it passes through Smithfield, a small river town that except for a couple of historic homes and an ancient inn is pretty much without distinction. Well, not quite. For within the corporate limits of the village, and nowhere else, are produced Smithfield hams, not just the finest hams in the United States but the best hams in the world. This statement is offered quietly, reasonably, and without qualification.

Good country hams, indeed extraordinary hams, can be gotten from small hog raisers and curers around the nearby towns of Suffolk, Surrey, and Sussex, and from one as far away as Richmond, and to a large extent they are smoked and dry-cured to the Smithfield formula. But the connoisseur of hams — like the wine expert who can distinguish from which side of the road in Saint-Emilion the wine came — insists that there are subtleties in the taste of the genuine Smithfield ham that sets it apart from all others.

Knowledgeable and cultivated people don't argue the point.

The dedication of gourmets to Smithfield ham is not blind stubbornness; after all, the hams have been cured that way since Captain John Smith and the original Jamestown settlers observed how the Indians smoked and cured venison, and decided to adapt the technique to pork products. If there was a better way of doing it, they argue, it would have come to light in the past two hundred and fifty years.

Just as the olive and garlic form the foundation of the cooking of Provence, the ham is the keystone of good southern cooking and all truly grand meals are built around it. What sets the Smithfield ham off from all others — from Yorkshire, Parma, Polish, *prosciutto, jambon de Bayonne*, and the hams of Tennessee, Georgia, and Missouri — is its taste and texture: it is slightly oily (an asset in a ham), firm, lean, and its taste is strong and more likely than not a bit salty. The oil originally came from peanuts, but economy in recent years has eliminated peanuts from the diet of hogs sold to the Smithfield processors. Now the hogs are turned loose to root for acorns and nuts in the forests, and they follow the harvesters into the peanut fields to take what's left. It seems to work. Almost all Smithfield hams come from hogs raised in southern Virginia, North and South Carolina, and Georgia, and none of them are exclusively corn-fed hogs. A diet of corn alone is no more likely to produce a good ham than a bad grape will produce a fine claret. It isn't in the cards. But the robust flavor of a fully aged, dry-cured Smithfield ham today is unchanged from that of a hundred years ago when Queen Victoria, whose opinions were scarcely humble ones, insisted that they be shipped to her regularly from Smithfield, Virginia, and

Sarah Bernhardt demanded that they be sent to her in Paris. Mrs. Woodrow Wilson presented one to Marshal Joffre, the World War I hero, when he visited the United States, and George Rector, one of America's greatest restaurateurs, solemnly declared the Smithfield ham to be the best in the world. This is a respectable body of opinion.

There are four producers of Smithfield hams now operating in the village and there aren't likely to be any more because the town's corporate boundaries are firmly set. Altogether they produce about 150,000 pieces a year; "piece" is a trade synonym for ham, and one hears it frequently around Smithfield. The largest producer is the Gwaltney Company, which in 1972 was bought out by — believe it or not — ITT. The others are the Smithfield Packing Company, locally known as Luter's since it is operated by J. W. Luter; Smithfield Ham and Products; and V. W. Joyner, which is now operated by Swift and Company. These four, and these alone, according to Virginia law can produce Smithfield hams, and all use precisely the same process. There are those who claim the ability to distinguish a Gwaltney ham from a Luter, say, in a blindfold test, but old-timers pay no attention to such nonsense. Howard Gwaltney, Sr., who retired from the Smithfield ham business a couple of years ago and who probably knows more about these pieces than anyone alive, shrugs this off with a laugh. "I can't tell the difference," he says. If he can't, it's doubtful that anyone can.

There is nothing remotely arcane about the processing of a Smithfield ham and none of the foolishness that soft-drink manufacturers delight in, with mysterious ingredients and formulas kept forever under lock and key. After a ham is selected to become a Smithfield ham, its processing is routine: it stays thirty-five days in salt, then twenty-one days in what is known as "equalization time" (when the salt is permitted to penetrate and equalize itself throughout the ham), then it is smoked with red oak or hickory for a period of five days, and rubbed with black pepper. It is then encased in loose-weave cloth and hung to be air-cured for a minimum of six months. At that point it may be sold. Further aging, however, is felt by many ham lovers to improve the taste. Some think eighteen months is ideal, others wouldn't dream of cooking a ham until it has hung for two years. The longer it hangs the stronger the taste becomes because moisture in the meat evaporates, and moisture keeps the taste mild. The average piece loses nearly 25 percent of its weight in the curing process and it will lose almost four ounces a month after it has been hung to age — all from moisture loss — but very lean hams will lose less. Moisture generally resides in the fat. A Gwaltney ham that was cured in 1934 was recently moved when Gwaltney's Smokehouse Number One was temporarily closed down. Its original weight at curing was 14 pounds 8 ounces. When weighed at the close of 1975 its weight had dropped to 6 pounds 4 ounces. Although the meat had in no sense spoiled, the ham was no longer edible. Wrinkled and the color of cordovan leather, it was so solid in texture that it would have been impossible at that time to soak out the salt. An even older Smithfield ham, the seventy-year-old "Methuselah," is now in the possession of Howard Gwaltney, Jr., a gift from his father. Like the younger 1934 ham, it has mummified in a way that would prevent it from ever being eaten.

Temperature means nothing in dry-curing or aging a ham. In the curing rooms of Smithfield, they hang in cotton bags at room temperature which, under the strong Virginia summer sun, means that the thermometer often hovers around a hundred degrees for days at a time. Hams that have been bought completely cured may be hung in a closet or in a kitchen indefinitely; freezing is bad but mold means nothing. Everybody in Smithfield has a story about how a person unfamiliar with hams went into shock upon discovering mold on a gift ham and promptly discarded it in the garbage. Some people insist that a partial coating of mold sharpens the flavor of a ham, but there is no evidence to prove this and the theory is generally discounted by people who know hams well. Mold should be washed off with a brush before the ham is soaked.

Since the Smithfield ham is felt to be the hog's greatest contribution to world gastronomy, only perfect hams are selected from the 35,000 hogs butchered each week in Smithfield for the fulfillment of this destiny. Those making the selection go largely by eye, looking for the proper size and freedom from blemish, but the iliac gland is the big tip-off to whether or not there is an internal bruise that may disqualify the piece. If the gland is dark or bloody that is considered ample evidence of a bruise, and the ham quickly falls from the assembly line. The only place where science falters is in the smokehouse. Here peculiar things happen. In four identical smoking rooms, all made of the same wood and at the same time, minor variations in smoking procedures must be made in each and nobody knows why. Experience has proved that hams must be held longer in some rooms than in others, but the reasons are shrouded in mystery and the men who operate the smokehouses have long ago run out of logical explanations. In any event, this aristocrat of hams is produced entirely by hand and by nature. No mechanization is involved, a circumstance that undoubtedly frustrated the ITT engineers when they first took over the Gwaltney business.

While the long shank and long butt are the hallmarks of the Smithfield ham, each of the four processors also produces a "country" or short-cured ham which would be called a Number Two grade anywhere else but which brings a shudder from the Smithfield people when the term is used. The Gwaltney country ham is called Williamsburg, while Luter and Joyner call theirs the Jamestown and the Red Eye respectively. Smithfield Ham and Products does not produce a country ham, but under the name of Amber they offer an impressive line of ham spreads and sliced ham in glass. But there is one notable difference between the lesser grade and the genuine Smithfield ham, in addition to size, contour, and price. While both are processed the same way to a point, the compact ham (it is not nearly as long as the Smithfield) is speeded up all along the way. Its equalization time is reduced to eighteen days, and it then goes into a heat cycle for four weeks, during which it is smoked for four days. The curing time is only eighty-four days, or twelve weeks, as opposed to the full six months required for the Smithfield label. Thus the fast-cured ham is slightly greener, but one can let it hang three or four months more in the kitchen and it will be very close to the real thing.

A final detail: the slicing of the cooked ham once it arrives at the table more than anything else separates the men from the boys. Howard Gwaltney, Sr., contends the slice must be thin, the thinner the better. "Use a very sharp knife," he advises, "and slice the ham so thin that you can see the shadow of the blade behind it."

INSTRUCTIONS FOR COOKING A
SMITHFIELD HAM

1. Soak the ham in cool, clear water for twelve hours, or longer if desired. Those objecting to a salty taste should soak the ham for twenty-four hours, changing the water at the halfway point.
2. Wash the ham thoroughly, scrubbing it with a stiff brush to remove all mold and pepper.
3. Place it in a pot skin down, and cover with cool water. Bring the water to 180° F. (not quite simmering), then cook for about twenty-five minutes per pound. Add water as needed to keep the ham covered. The pot should be covered.
4. When the ham is done, lift it from the pot and remove skin and fat (if desired) while it is still warm.
5. If a sweet coating is desired, score the ham, cover it with brown sugar, and bake it in an oven at 400° F. for fifteen minutes.

WARNING: Do not cut the ham before cooking, but cook whole. This keeps the juices in.

HOWARD GWALTNEY'S FAVORITE
SMITHFIELD HAM CASSEROLE

Cut off a few fairly thick large slices and place them in the bottom of a casserole. Cover with about one inch of cooked crabmeat. Add a top layer of ham slices, and bake for about twenty minutes at 350° F., or until the red-eye gravy from the ham mixes thoroughly with the crabmeat. Serve hot.

3

Arriving in Europe on a Night Flight

I COME off the plane and walk through the maze of corridors that lead to Passport Control and Baggage Delivery and Customs. A cautious wave of excitement lifts me momentarily, a reflexive response to arrival in Europe, and then deposits me again on the shelf of fatigue and torpor. The woman walking on my right pauses at a corner and studies the directional signs. Her face possesses that numb and disengaged expression, the look of a person who has slept poorly if at all. I am aware that I wear that expression too, the eyes not believing what they see, the ears ringing faintly. The signs that say AUSGANG and USCITA and SORTIE and EXIT make uneven contact with my reasoning mind like a faulty telephone connection. I know what all the words mean — they mean the same and they will eventually deliver me out of the terminal — but now the windows of my mind are clouded like an ancient mirror.

In the queue at Passport Control I glance at my wristwatch; it is nearly two o'clock in the morning in New York, but a ceiling clock proclaims the local time as three minutes to eight. The passport officer glances at my photograph, glances at me, recognizes a tolerable similarity, stamps the passport, and hands it to me. A man behind me says something in German to the passport officer and then laughs heartily, but the latter seems less amused than annoyed. I glance behind and see the officer with his hands resting on the counter, his fingers laced together. He unclasps his hands, takes the man's passport, stamps it and returns it without speaking. Eight o'clock is too early for jokes.

It makes no difference if one has arrived at a flughaven or aeroporte or aeroporto or airport, the new terminals of Europe are alike early in the morning. There are the long, glistening, highly waxed corridors, the hurrying groups, the ghostly announcements echoing along the passages and intended for — whom? One is fortunate if a WECHSEL–CHANGE–CAMBIO sign is lighted; it is early for moneychangers to be working. But one can buy the *Frankfurter Zeitung* or *L'Express* or the *Stockholm Tagblatt* at a newsstand, or liquor or sweaters or neckties or cameras or calculators, paying dollars and taking local currency in return. The exchange is unfavorable but it is all right for small amounts. Early morning delivery of baggage is slow — Rome's Fiumicino is the slowest of all — and I drop into a chair in a small café and, waving aside the menu, ask in English for a coffee and a croissant. In French the waiter inquires if I also want *confiture* and in English I say yes. He disappears, and in seconds returns and places the breakfast before me. The coffee is hot and strong, and tastes the way European coffee always tastes, a singularly European taste. In some European cities, especially Florence, the odor of coffee hangs in the air over the whole city, never entirely disappearing. I lean back against the plastic cushion and manage to get my legs crossed under the miniature table. A middle-aged man in a trench coat takes a seat at a table next to me. He unbuttons the coat and I see he is wearing a muffler around his neck and that he has on a sweater under his suit jacket: the uniform of the middle-class European businessman. He makes a signal to the waiter — no words are spoken — and he is brought a cup of coffee and a small glass of brandy. He pours the brandy into the coffee and tastes it tentatively; Europeans and most notably the French are suspicious of the quality of anything to be eaten or drunk. He seems satisfied, and takes a newspaper from his trench-coat pocket and spreads it open on the table. The newspaper is *Le Monde*.

It is still early. I join a small group of stragglers moving down a corridor marked *Livraison des Bagages*. Under the bright fluorescent glare we all look rumpled and cross. One man is eating a cheese sandwich whose parched corners are lifted; his heart clearly isn't in it and he keeps looking around for a trash receptacle. At the end of the corridor there is a departure gate for a Lufthansa flight to Nairobi. A small, silent group of people are waiting for someone to arrive to check them in; they look more like businessmen than safari adventurers. We come at last to the baggage carousels, and I spot my suitcase instantly. As I wait for it to come around, an expensive blue suitcase passes that has broken open, prompting a lady beside me to cluck sympathetically. I lift my bag from the belt, shrug off the help of a porter, and follow an arrow that points to ZOLL, DOUANE, CUSTOMS. An agent scrawls an indecipherable chalk mark on my bag and wearily gestures me through. I have arrived.

It is curious how the ritual of arriving in Europe carries with it that slightly submerged feeling of anticipation, that strange spark of excitement. It is almost invariably there, whether the arrival is the first or the fifteenth, and only those who are hopelessly jaded or totally preoccupied by business fail to feel it. The first rush of sensations — advertisements for Byrrh, the sound of motor scooters, butter in hollow scoops on silver trays, *fruits de mer* on the menu — speak of Europe and no place else. Here one is on the edge of adventure, whether it dies stillborn or not. I think the second arrival is more exciting perhaps than the first, partly because the edge of anxiety accompanying a strange experience is blunted and one knows, in the main, what to expect.

Outside I surrender my bag to a porter and crawl wearily into a bus that will take me into the city. The windshield wipers are moving like metronomes, the inside of the glass is fogged by human breath. Why is it always raining when one arrives in a European city? I stare bleakly out the window, after clearing a small area with my elbow. I see large directional signs to the city, two foreign airline maintenance structures, and, through the mist, an anonymous factory, its single smokestack pouring a column of dirty, brown smoke into the sky. Up close, beside the bus, there are advertisements exhorting me to attend a concert, to visit Corsica for ten sun-filled, fun-filled days, to buy a Phillips razor, and to drink Punt e Mes. An electric sign, glowing bright under the heavy overcast, suggests I fly home by British Airways. The first sights of Europe.

The doors close with the sound of air escaping, and the bus crawls away from the terminal. It is raining quite hard now; a man on a motorcycle has stopped to adjust his rain gear. There is very little traffic; a few trucks pass the bus, sending a spray of water across the windshield. We cross a bridge, and through the gray mist below I can see a tug pulling a string of barges. The river, the bridge, the sky, and the buildings are all of one color; Europe summons up its sounds, smells, contours, and textures in many sensual ways but its color in the rain is immutable gray. One crosses a bridge to get to all European cities, I don't know why.

Inside the city, the bus slows and slips into the stream of traffic. We pass a small park, which is deserted in the early morning rain; the chairs of the café are upended on the tables. A circular flower bed provides the only color in the landscape's monotone, bright red geraniums that seem almost iridescent. The streets now are via or calle or rue or something-strasse, and the shops have unfamiliar names. The sidewalks are moving streams of umbrellas. A lighted digital clock in a bank advertisement gives the time as 8:56 and the temperature as 49 degrees. Cold and raw. The bus pulls into the driveway of a hotel and stops. The doors open.

The lobby is brightly lit, cheerful, and full of motion, as in all large European hotels. At reception, as I fill out the endless registration form that seeks to learn, among many other things, my passport number and the date and place of issue. I inquire if I can still get *service d'étage* or *servizio ai piani* and I am told, politely but sternly, that room service is always available. I am rebuked, but I don't mind. I have forgotten; this is not an American hotel that offers only shelter. I stop at the newsstand and get a copy of the *Paris Herald-Tribune* and follow the porter to the elevator. A well-dressed woman is waiting there, a tower of worldliness and sophistication. She regards me frankly and without embarrassment but her face does not change its expression. When the door opens she steps briskly in without another glance at me, and I enter behind her. The door shuts, and the elevator moves upward. I am in Europe.

4

Europe's Most European Country

i.

For anyone seeking tranquillity, or some greater or lesser prize, it seems to me that the foolproof place is Switzerland. This tiny country, one-half the size of South Carolina, brings together the activist and the idler, the recluse and the rover, the adventurer and the dreamer. It possesses the most comfortable hotels in the world, and although as a sports arena it is unequaled anywhere, it demands nothing of its guests except solvency. It has always been this way, cheerfully exchanging privacy and comfort for what the Swiss consider more material symbols of contentment. One reads the history of Switzerland and finds the pages blank; as a nation it has done nothing and prospered while others supported armies and navies and made war. For what it's good at, it cannot be surpassed.

I had been to Geneva a number of times, as well as to Lausanne, Zurich and other Swiss cities, and had drawn from the visits only the impression that of all the countries of Europe, Switzerland was the most totally European. But it was not until I left the cities and went to San Bernardino, the village that nestles in the pass leading to the lakes and to

Italy, that I discovered the extraordinary flavor of the country and the true personality of the Swiss. San Bernardino is in the canton of Grisons, which claims the stylish winter resorts of Saint Moritz, Klosters, and Davos, but it is far less modish than its chic neighbors and, in fact, is even a bit tacky. I first visited the pass in the early autumn, arriving from Chur by Swiss Postal Bus, which in itself was a sheer delight, and settling at the Hotel Bocce e Poste. It was one of those small but extraordinarily snug Swiss hotels, with lots of sunlight spilling into the lobby, a cheerful dining room and bar, and the whole staff, minute as it was, enormously eager to please.

I was served some fine *torte di formaggio*, smooth-tasting cheese tarts, in a room adjoining the lobby before dinner, together with a glass of Fendant, the white, crisp, uncomplicated wine by which the entire country seems to be irrigated. Dinner that night consisted of venison stew, and with it a red wine called Merlot, a product of the Italian-speaking canton of Ticino. A total stillness lay upon the village when I went to my room after dinner; my last recollection was seeing a small shaft of moonlight on the wall as I burrowed under the eiderdown. Visitors and money are well cared for by the Swiss.

The San Bernardino Pass strikes one as an exceptional achievement in mountain design. Looking from my window the next morning, I saw that the valley between the peaks was laid out neatly behind the village, with the awesome cliff face of Piz Uccelos dominating the scene. The mountain got its name, I was told, because birds fleeing the cold of northern Europe and the fretful Alpine winds used the pass as a means of getting to the Mediterranean and North Africa. Some Swiss friends had arranged a picnic for me on a high Alpine plateau, and the day was tailored for the occasion. Leaving the village on foot, we crossed a dam which backed up water to form an artificial lake, and entered the forest. The path rose moderately, I was pleased to discover, and through the tops of the trees I could see snow that had lain on the peaks throughout the summer. Although it was September and the sun was warm in the open spots, the air had a cutting edge in the spruce forest and I was glad to slip on my jacket over my sweater. Wild raspberries and blueberries grew along the path. I fell to eating them ravenously, one of the marvels of the twentieth century being the extent to which modern growing methods have robbed commercial fruit and berries of their flavor. The high meadows, when we arrived, were as silent as the forest since the cowbells had been stilled when the cows — like the birds — had moved south for the winter.

The hut that was to be the site of our picnic appeared suddenly at the edge of the forest, in a meadow that was totally flat, utterly empty, and astonishingly beautiful. A farmer lived upstairs, while on the ground floor four pigs slumbered contentedly in one room, and cows, ducks, and chickens inhabited another. A chained dog barked a few times, but it was mostly for the record; when I approached him he wagged his tail vigorously and showed every sign of wanting to join the picnic as an active guest. Beside a concrete trough overflowing with spring water, a table had been set up, covered with a gingham cloth, and on it were great quantities of *prosciutto cotto*, fat local salami, large wheels of *formaggio dell'Alpe* (cheese made in the farmer's hut), loaves of coarse bread, and a cask of Barbera, a clear, red wine from the Piedmont of Italy. A Swiss girl playfully threw a handful of wild blueberries in my glass of wine,

[34]

and I left them there. The wine was new — perhaps from the grapes which had just been gathered — and it was full, fruity, and totally lacking in aristocracy. I felt it was just right for the occasion.

A few days later and I am at Ascona, a small town bordering Lake Maggiore near the Italian frontier. A friend drives me high into the Valle Verzasca to a small village called Sonogno. It is a town lifted undisturbed from Swiss calendar art: stone houses decorated with window boxes of geraniums, winding streets, blue sky, and towering peaks. From somewhere my friend has produced a bicycle. "It's eighteen miles to the foot of the pass but it's all downhill," he says. "I'll be there to meet you. When you come to the village of San Bartolomeo pull into the churchyard. There will be a surprise for you."

I set out on the most exhilarating ride I have ever experienced. It was not yet noon, the sun was warm, the road was empty, and I coasted grandly. The village of Frasco fell behind me, and then Gerra. At times the peaks came down to a point only wide enough for the road to slip through, and at other times mountain streams raced along the road beside me. The wind whistled in my ears, and for the first time in years I had the ridiculous urge to sing. Brione was a larger village than the others, so I braked to a safe speed, but from there to Motta I eased up on the brake and soared. At San Bartolomeo, I pulled into the churchyard and was delighted to find that my friend had left me a basket filled with salami, bread and wine. I sat in the grass in the sunlight and feasted. He was waiting for me at Vogorno, beside a stream the color of the sky, and I reluctantly got into his car. What a way to see a country!

ii.

A WINE-TASTING in America is often more comic than enjoyable, largely because Americans have not yet learned to relax around wine. In this country, wine is a test of sophistication, and one's worldliness is measured by one's knowledge of vineyards, of labels, of vintages. When the door to social salvation is thus opened by a little knowledge of wine, those who pass through will do so uneasily, never certain that they know enough and always predisposed to pretend they know a little more than they do. The wine-tastings that I have attended in New York and California have been, for the most part, needlessly stuffy and unbending, with wines invariably described in terms of human behavior. "I doubt that it ever had a chance," I once heard a guest say solemnly at a wine-tasting in the St. Regis Hotel in New York. "It was smothered in infancy."

The most pleasant and informative wine-tasting I can remember occurred in Sion, in the heart of Switzerland's chief wine-producing region. This area, known as the Valais, produces more than a third of all Swiss wine and nowhere are there such a wide variety of grapes grown as in the Valais. But what sets a Swiss wine-tasting apart is the totally relaxed manner the Swiss maintain toward their wines; they avoid the religious fervor of the French, the apologetic disdain of the Italians, and the institutional anxiety of the Germans. In Switzerland a wine is a beverage, nothing more, and the hell with its breeding. Aristocracy is less important than availability. The Swiss like dry wines, but if only sweet wines are available, they will be drunk and no complaints voiced. I once asked a Swiss wine producer if he thought wine was a healthy drink, and he replied promptly and without guile. "Wine is fine if you drink it regularly," he said, "but don't drink it irregularly too much." It was an awkward statement, but I knew what he meant.

Late one afternoon in November I was invited to a wine-tasting in the caves of Provins, the wine cooperative of the Valais. There were seven guests, all Americans, and as we were ushered into the windowless room and told to take seats at a large table, our host sought to put us at ease. The main thing was to enjoy the wine, we were told; all questions would be answered but the gathering of information was to be a secondary consideration.

Of the wines of the Valais, he said in a brief introduction, two-thirds are white, and one-third red. One of the most popular is Fendant, which possesses about 13 Oechsle degrees. An Oechsle degree is a measure of the sugar content of a wine. Sweet wines have a much higher sugar content. From 45 to 48 percent of all Valais production is in Fendant, which has extremely low acidity. The Greeks originally brought the grapes to the area, and Swiss grapes are generally healthy and vigorous.

Our host then directed that the first wine be poured. It was Fendant Pierrefeu 1974. "Sip it if you wish," he said, "or drink it all. We observe no set rules here. We do not believe the nonsense about rotating red wines clockwise in the mouth and white wines counterclockwise. Taste it any way that suits you best."

I had drunk a lot of Fendant since I had been in Switzerland and I like it. This was a good Fendant; no better than others I had had and no worse either. The next wine, also white, was a Johannisberg Rhonegold 1973, made from a Sylvaner grape found mostly in Germany and Austria. It was better than the Fendant.

"Remember that Swiss wines are drunk while young,

especially the white wines," our host explained. "There is not a great difference between one vintage and another. There are differences, but there is more equilibrium among our wines than in other countries."

The next three wines poured, all white, were Arvine Vieux Pays 1970, Ermitage Les Chapelles 1973, and Malvoisie Roxene 1973. The Arvine was a little sharp, and the Ermitage, whose plants originally came from the Côtes du Rhône, was too bland for my taste. The Malvoisie was pleasant and refreshing. A Pinot, older than the Pinot Noir, the Malvoisie plants were brought to Switzerland in the seventeenth century. It was a very dry wine and was said to possess the most acidity of any wine produced in the Valais.

After drinking the white wines, all the glasses were rinsed in red wine, which was poured from glass to glass and eventually into a pitcher. Wine is a better rinsing agent than water, and wine authorities recoil from the thought of water splashing about in wine glasses. There were two red wines: Dole Chanteauvieux 1966 and Pinot Noir 1971. The Dole, our host said, could be either pure Pinot Noir or a blend of Pinot Noir and Gamay, and the law required that it be at least 8.5 Oechsle degrees. The Dole is usually drunk quite young, so a 1966 is considered rather old. In making the Dole, we were told, the grapes are taken from the stem, unlike Bordeaux, and have much less tannin as a result. The tannin in Bordeaux requires four years or more for taste removal, but since there is less tannin in Dole there is no barrier to its being drunk young. I preferred the Dole to the Pinot Noir, which had a sharp aftertaste and left my teeth coated.

"In the Valais we have very little precipitation," our host said, "and we must use artificial irrigation by bringing water from the mountains. Since water accounts for acidity, other countries have too much acidity and we have the opposite problem — not enough. Perhaps these differences make for interesting wines."

I poured a half glass of Pinot Noir into the pitcher, and rinsed my glass with Fendant. I asked if I might try again the Johannisberg. Our host seemed pleased and filled my glass to the top. "Since the tasting is over," he said, smiling, "you are free to drink your favorites." The Johannisberg, I decided, was too sweet for sustained drinking, but it was the most pleasant of the seven wines served us.

Later that evening, I climbed the hill toward the old fort in search of the ancient cellar restaurant that specialized in raclette, the traditional Swiss dinner of melted cheese, boiled potato, and gherkins. I took a seat in a dim corner of the restaurant, and by the flickering light of a candle I examined the menu. A girl in a checkered dress and apron stood in front of me with a pad.

"I'll have raclette," I said.

"Et votre vin?" she inquired.

I thought a moment, but just a moment.

"Fendant," I replied, handing her the menu.

iii.

PONTRESINA and Saint Moritz are so close as to be almost one, but the former is a very small and rather modest village while the other is, well, Saint Moritz. A deep valley, Val Roseg, extends almost directly north from Pontresina, with the Rosatsch mountain on the right and the Morteratsch on the left, and it comes to a dead end at the far end, where another awesome range begins. I have seen the Val Roseg only once — in the dead of winter when snow lay everywhere — and I saw it then under such strange and ghostly circumstances that my judgment is not to be totally trusted, but I have the impression that the entire valley is nothing but a trail cut through the forest, a few bridges where the trail apparently crosses mountain streams, and absolutely nothing else. Nothing that is, except that at the far end of the valley there is a restaurant called the Roseg Glacier Restaurant, but I never heard it referred to as anything other than "the restaurant." I can't tell you where its customers are drawn from as it is as remote as anything you can possibly imagine, nestled there by the glacier at the end of the valley and eight miles from Pontresina, which is the nearest village. I went there one night in a horse-drawn sleigh with seven other people, and if there is any other way of getting there I don't want to know about it.

There were two sleighs, enormous things of a style one associates with Czarist Russia, and I must acknowledge that I approached the venture with some misgiving because it was a brutally cold night and eight miles is a distance not accomplished quickly in a sleigh. I faced forward, although two of the benches faced the rear and were probably warmer, and just before we took off the driver threw sheepskins over us all. Although they shed in a way I have never seen a skin molt, they cut out the cold night air. We started.

Dreams have a way of attaching bits of reality, as well as the reverse, so I am not at all certain what happened that night. There was a full moon, which in itself added a great element of mystery to the snowy valley, and I was aware of a landscape of strange and beautiful things moving past the sleigh. Conversation in the sleigh soon stopped, and the only sound was the heavy breathing of the horses and the song of the runners moving over the snow. I remember we were in the forest quite a long time, and then emerged into a cleared area where we crossed a bridge. The valley floor was level and the sleigh moved swiftly. Occasionally shadowy bulges seemed to move in the distance, but I doubt that they really did. In the daylight they would probably have been large rocks or stunted spruce trees, but they added another haunting note to the symphony of that odd and dreamy night.

I don't know how long we had been moving, more than an hour at least, when cold began to creep in under the sheepskins. The two sleighs had separated and I was in the rear one, but about a half-hour later I heard shouting ahead and reasoned that the occupants of the first sleigh had seen the lights of the restaurant. I was right. We sped over a small bridge, the driver cranking the brake to keep the sleigh from getting too close to the horses, and a slight distance ahead of us was the restaurant. I don't remember throwing off the sheepskins or stumbling into the building, but I remember the bright glare as I entered the room, I saw a huge fire in the fireplace, I heard accordion music, and someone placed a *boccalino* of wine in my hand.

Later, at a long table, we were served a steaming risotto, with bottles of wine being passed up and down, and a pleasant fuzziness began to blur the evening's events. There was dancing, much singing, and it was quite late when we piled out of the restaurant and got back in the sleighs. For some reason, the trip back to Pontresina seemed much quicker than the trip to the restaurant. There was singing in the sleighs, some occasionally on key, and several bottles of wine moved about under the sheepskins.

iv.

THE greatest institution ever devised for the comfort and well-being of the human being is the Swiss hotel. I've stayed in many fine hotels that were not in Switzerland, but almost invariably lurking somewhere in the background were either some Swiss workers or, more likely, a Swiss manager, or almost certainly someone who was trained for hotel work in Switzerland. Where most people think of Switzerland as one giant *horlogerie*, I think of it as an enormous hotel with rooms of various prices and appointments but all of them good.

Perhaps the most notable thing about the Swiss hotel, whether large or small, is the churchlike silence that prevails in the corridors and guest rooms. What sounds that are occasionally heard are muffled and indistinct, and seem to come from far away. I know the hallways are carpeted and quite often the guest rooms have double doors, and these deaden sound considerably, but there must be something more that I don't know about. But just that lovely quietness is reassuring, and gives a guest a feeling of snugness; I feel cared for immediately.

When I think of a Swiss hotel, I think of wide marble stairs leading from the lobby to the upper floors, but these, too, are carpeted, and there is always some sort of surprising public room on the second floor. It may be a reading room, or a breakfast room, or a cardroom, but there will be something there that will make the investigation worthwhile. When one comes in at night, the bed is neatly prepared and a small white towel has been placed on top of the rug at bedside. On the bed, in place of a blanket, is a thick eiderdown, absurdly light in weight but very warm and inviting. There are pull curtains to keep out the morning sun, and they are heavy, lined, and often velvet. The bathroom is almost as big as the bedroom and contains a tub that a six-footer can stretch out in. Beside the tub is a pull chain to summon the maid, for what purpose I can't imagine but it's inevitably there. There is a small wicker table beside the basin, and on this each day is spread a clean white towel. On it one places one's toilet articles.

I think of the hushed hallways, and tea being served in cheerful lobbies during the afternoon, and doors that fit precisely and window clasps that function effortlessly, the concierge who knows everything, and the desk clerk who knows *almost* everything, and the fresh flowers on every table, and the paintings that are not reproductions of Van Gogh's *Drawbridge at Arles*. I think of the faceless man in the green apron who shines shoes left in the hallway during the night and who is occasionally surprised by an early riser. I can't emphasize the wonder and delight of a stairway that leads sensibly to the lobby and not to some labyrinthine destination under the garage. There are the cheerful chandeliers at twilight, the quiet courtesy of the waiter who brings you a cup of hot chocolate and who has enough sense to find you although you are no longer sitting where you were when you gave him the order, of the total privacy you can enjoy in the lobby if that is your wish.

I think of the bottle of mineral water brought as speedily to a guest room at midnight as it would be in midafternoon, of the porter who comes instantly for your bags, which he carefully straps together, of the forwarding address taken as seriously as a trust, and the slightly stricken feeling one experiences in getting in the departing taxicab.

I was marooned in a heavy snowstorm not long ago in a small hotel in Villars, a tiny town high in the Alpes Vaudoises above Lake Geneva, and while I am certain that a determined effort could have gotten me safely down to Montreux, I had not the slightest inclination to make the effort. It snowed without stopping for three days and as far as I was concerned it was three days of sheer delight.

I pulled the curtains back on the first morning and gazed into a gray nothingness. The mountains, the village, even the park in front of the hotel, had disappeared behind a curtain of snow. I pushed open the window and stuck out my hand and the flakes touched my skin daintily but there was a businesslike threat in the air and the sky was heavily overcast. Downstairs, I had breakfast beside a window and watched the skiers stamp off to buses, and then the buses, one by one, pulled away from the hotel entrance and were swallowed up in the snow. After breakfast, I put on boots and started to walk to the village. A Fiat was trying unsuccessfully to get up the hill to the hotel entrance, then the driver abandoned the effort and started backing downhill. In the village there were few cars and I walked in the street until I found a konditorei. My cap, my muffler and my coat gave off a small blizzard when I shook them, and I stamped the snow from my boots. The windows were steamed up, so I sat at a table in the rear and ordered a cup of tea. The waitress remarked that there was *beaucoup de neige* and I replied that there was *encore neige dans le ciel*, and we both smiled.

Back at the hotel, the older guests who had spent the morning over coffee in the lobby and gossiping about the storm regarded me as an adventurer from another world when I returned. I did not dwell excessively upon the ease of my expedition. Life in the lobby had suddenly become clublike; guests talked who had never before spoken to each other, glasses of cognac were tipped to each other's health, every scrap of information, however questionable, about driving conditions was passed quickly about, an air of relaxation prevailed. Later that night, I filled up the great tub with hot water and soaked awhile. Aside from my own splashing, there was no sound in either the bathroom or the bedroom. After I dried off, I opened the steamed window and looked out. Great, feathery flakes fell on the window-sill. I closed the window and got into bed. There is no place in the world where one can wait out a snowstorm as comfortably as a Swiss hotel.

5

The Hotel in a Cave

In the Tunisian desert, not far from the oasis of Gabès, the mountains of Matmata overlook a strange valley that resembles nothing so much as the surface of the moon. This sun-baked saucer of ocher-colored earth is relieved only by an occasional date palm and the pockmarks of hundreds of deep pits, in which Berber families — modern troglodytes — have made their homes. It is here, on this baking plain, that two hotels — the Marhala and the Sidi Driss — have been carved out of the earth to provide cool, subterranean rooms for travelers. It's an odd experience to sleep in a cave, with the bedstead and night table chiseled out of hard clay, but it isn't unpleasant.

My opinion of caves, admittedly aprioristic, was that they were cold, damp, dark and filled with crawling things. I had arranged to visit a troglodyte family out of sheer and unalloyed curiosity, and I was astounded to find, when I arrived, that the family dwelling was well lighted, dry, spotlessly clean and from all appearances quite comfortable. The Berber wife, who shyly showed me around her cave, spoke no English but obviously possessed pride in her living room, which was lighted by a large airshaft, and especially in her kitchen, with rows of pots resting on a clay shelf. Seated on a rug on the floor of the living room, I drank a cup of unsweetened tea and discussed the return to Gabès with the man who had brought me from the oasis. The thought of the searing drive back across the wadis, under the desert sun, was not tempting and I had suggested we tarry with the troglodytes until late in the afternoon. It was then that he told me about the hotel, which he said was quite close by. Perhaps, he said, I would care to spend the night there, and leave early in the morning for the trip back to Gabès. I assented instantly.

It's difficult to explain the architectural dynamics of a hotel cave but I'll try. First, imagine a group of, say, five circular pits in the ground, each of which is about thirty feet across and about thirty feet deep. The pits are connected by tunnels to link the structure together, but the basic function of the pits is to provide daylight and ventilation for the underground rooms, all of which open on the pits. Caves, or rooms, are on two levels, and all are hollowed out of the earth. The rooms are clean and dry, and most of those I saw contained a bed against each of two walls, a shelf or bed table between the beds, and a skin or rug on the floor. Wooden doors provide privacy and protection, and that's about it. No, there's something else. The top story, if that's what it is, is reached by stairs cut out of the wall of the pit, with the exception of a few rooms that are arrived at by climbing hand over hand up a knotted rope. Baggage is tossed up, and down. Since there is no electricity, the rooms are lighted by candles. High-strung chaps looking under the bed for scorpions are surprised to find there is nothing to look under. The mattresses rest on solid earthen benches.

My companion from Gabès showed great distaste for the

whole hotel as the manager showed us around, and his ill-concealed displeasure turned to bewilderment when I selected a room reached by mounting a rope. He obviously thought I was crazy. I climbed up easily — there were indentations cut into the wall for the feet — and a few moments later my flight bag was tossed up to me. I left the door open for light, took a few items out of the bag and arranged them on the bed table, then swung down again (it was a little trickier than coming up), and went to the manager's office at the entrance to the cave. My companion had departed for Gabès, the manager said, but would return early the next morning and left word for me to be ready to leave by six o'clock.

The manager showed me the location of the toilet, the least attractive feature of the entire place, and later, on my own, I located the bar. It was a long, narrow cave, much darker than the others, with rugs and cushions lining the walls. It was lighted by candles and was empty but for the bartender. I sank down on a pillow with my back against the wall, and ordered a gin and tonic. It came without ice, but it was drinkable. A radio, somewhere behind the bar, was broadcasting popular music, with announcements in French. It was cool and pleasant, and after a while I ordered a second drink.

Some time later, the manager came to the bar to tell me it was time for dinner and offered to escort me to the *salle à manger*. This turned out to be a fairly large cave, not far from the main entrance, containing a long refectory table, already laid out with tableware and napkins, and perhaps a dozen chairs. One person, a swarthy, heavily bearded man, was already seated and was noisily eating soup. There were rugs and wall hangings to lighten the gloom of the room, and there were candles on the table as well as in wall brackets. The manager sat beside me, but made no effort to introduce me to the bearded man, who had finished his soup and was regarding me curiously. For some reason, I gathered we were the only guests in the hotel.

The hotel received few tourists, the manager said, and its guests were mostly business people traveling from Gabès to Tozeur or Nefta, two other oases, or to Medenine in the south. Recently, he continued, a few tourists had shown up, coming, like me, out of curiosity. The same was true of the Sidi Driss Hotel, which was nearby. "Tourists are uneasy about spending the night in the desert," he said. "There are scorpions, of course, but there are scorpions in the oases, and for that matter everywhere in North Africa. We search our rooms very carefully, and there are few places in which scorpions can hide. Tourists also like excitement, and there is very little of that we can offer."

Dinner was simple. The bread was fresh and the wine was fair. The soup, called *lebabli*, was made of chickpeas but was so loaded with garlic that I could taste little else. The main course was a couscous flavored with a meat that I finally concluded was mutton, but about which some doubt still lingers. For dessert, I had pitted dates, which were fresh and excellent. The manager asked if I would accept, with his compliments, a small glass of *boukha*, or fig liqueur, but I declined and asked if, instead, I could take a bottle of mineral water with me to my room. He waved his hand generously, and I selected a bottle from the table, making sure it was not Ain Oktor, which I had discovered early in Tunisia was more than slightly laxative. I stuffed the bottle in my belt when I climbed the rope to my room. It was easy.

I came down later to clean my teeth and take a shower. The water was rain stored in a cistern and it was clean and presumably safe. The shower was little more than a steady leak, but it was cooling and I felt refreshed when I had dried myself. Since it was still early, I decided to look around outside. There was a sliver of moon in the southern sky, but the night was quite dark. I could make out the huddled forms of several camels tethered near the entrance, and two men in robes sitting silently by a small fire. A teenage boy ran up to me and said something in Arabic, but I didn't understand him and waved him away. The landscape, when my eyes adjusted to the darkness, was unbelievably stark and unreal. There were strange little hills that loomed like black shadows, and etched on the horizon were a few date palms. There was nothing else. The air had turned cool and I shivered. I still don't know why deserts reach such extremes of temperature. I wandered a few hundred yards from the hotel, but there was something ghostly and unsettling about the terrain and I returned quickly. The manager wished me good night as I passed his office. He was reading a newspaper by the light of an oil lamp.

I awoke at daylight, dressed, and went down the rope. It was easier now that I had gotten the hang of it. I was surprised to see the manager in his office. The dining room was not yet officially open, he said, but there was some fruit and coffee for me there. I found a basket containing figs, dates, and — unbelievably — an apricot. The coffee was thick, black, very hot and very strong.

When I wandered back to the office, my driver was there, anxious to leave. It was going to be very hot, he said, and the sooner we left, the better. I went back to my room, got my bag, and stopped at the office to pay my bill. The room and two meals came to less than ten dollars. I shook hands with the manager and thanked him for his hospitality. He assured me that I was always welcome. Then, proudly, he added that there was a telephone in his office and I could call anytime for a booking.

6

Black Sand, Volcanoes
and the Sulfur Bath

I sat alone in the darkness in a tiny plane on the airstrip at Vieux Fort, waiting for a pilot to come to fly me to the other end of St. Lucia. A shower had just swept the airfield; the runway glistened, and the air was warm and moist. It was quiet except for the sound of night frogs, a high-pitched whine that in the nights to come on St. Lucia I scarcely noticed but which then struck me as plangent. Still, it was not an unpleasant sound, and I let the plane door remain open. I could tell I was near the sea — there was that unmistakable heavy sea smell in the air — but I could see nothing but stars and a few lights shining in the terminal building. I sat there for a half-hour before the pilot arrived, and I thought that perhaps this was a fine way to approach a new place. It allowed time for wonder to grow, for curiosity to sharpen . . .

You can tour the capital city of Castries on foot, I learned early the next morning, once you've gotten the hang of looking for traffic approaching from a strange direction. St. Lucians drive on the left, and I had a couple of close calls before I could readjust my reflexes. There are cities like Castries scattered all through the West Indies — small, hot, bustling waterfront towns — and while this one is no more attractive than the others, it is made more so by the St. Lucians themselves. During a morning of moving through the shops, the markets, the town square and a pause for a drink at La Dainty Bar — who could resist such a name? — I found none of the sullenness or resentment encountered by visitors on so many Caribbean islands. Perhaps this is because St. Lucia has not lost its identity and become foreign to its own inhabitants, a circumstance that has afflicted other islands in their unswerving obsession with tourism.

While English is the language of the island, most natives also speak a patois that is a curious mixture of French and African elements closely resembling the Creole of Haiti. This patois is an unwritten language and, I believe, it would be hell for an adult to learn. But it is beautiful when spoken, and I'm told that even upper-class St. Lucians slip into it when speaking intimacies.

Facts, mostly geographical:

St. Lucia is a small island in the Windward Group, twenty-seven miles long by fourteen miles at its widest point. It is located twenty-one miles south of the French island of Martinique, which is much bigger, and 110 miles northwest of Barbados, which is slightly smaller. On a clear day Martinique is an easily distinguishable landmass across the St. Lucia Channel, while from the southern end of the island one can easily see St. Vincent. The St. Vincent Passage is a witch's brew of crosscurrents, which makes sailing rough but doesn't deter boat traffic in either direction in the slightest. Politically, St. Lucia is an Associated State of

Great Britain, with a governor appointed by the Crown and a premier elected by the people. It is the premier who has the muscle.

The currency of St. Lucia is the East Caribbean dollar, which as I write is equal to approximately fifty cents in U.S. money. This two-for-one ratio makes for easy calculation, and American money is widely accepted throughout the island on that basis.

I can take some Caribbean islands and leave others alone, but after a few days in St. Lucia I realized I had lost my heart unashamedly there. The vegetation in the jungles and mountains is dizzying to the eyes; even in the villages the walls are buried in bougainvillea, in climbing flowers of all kinds; great lilies and hibiscus grow in profusion; giant taro leaves spring up from the banks of streams, and there are banana trees everywhere. On the drive south from Castries toward Soufrière, there are banana plantations in the valleys that offer such an explosion of greenery that it is almost overdone. On my first trip down the Caribbean coast, I came around a sharp curve and gazed down into a valley, and in the first minute I felt I had never seen anything more beautiful. In two minutes I had shifted into low gear. In three minutes I was looking for a place to park.

In Castries, I stayed at La Toc, a lovely hotel on a fine beach a mile or so from town. It would have been an excellent hotel anywhere, but it fitted the small cove nicely and seemed appropriate where it was. From time to time I went into town for dinner, but without exception I found the local restaurants mediocre or worse. One evening I sat on the small verandah of Coal Pot, a restaurant on the water's edge, and had a warmwater lobster and watched the waves skim across the sand almost beneath me. The menu offered snapper creole, shrimp creole and lobster. The *Callaloo* soup was excellent but otherwise the meal was distinguished by nothing except a surprisingly large check. For dessert I was offered banana flambée, which I rejected out of hand, having learned long ago that anything flambée was most likely something to watch and not to eat.

One day I drove north of Castries to Pigeon Island, which no longer is an island at all, having been joined to the mainland by a causeway. The landscape in this area is vastly different from that elsewhere on the island; it is more open, more cultivated, and boasts the only good road I saw on St. Lucia. There are several good hotels on this end of the island and passably good beaches. But candor compels me to say that the southern end of St. Lucia is more to my liking, so I will not dwell excessively on what lies north of Castries.

Marigot Bay, about midway between Castries and Soufrière, is a strikingly tropical extravaganza. A magnificent natural harbor almost entirely encircled by mountains dropping sharply to the sea, it is rimmed with coconut palms and possesses the bluest water that can be found in the Caribbean. Although Marigot Bay was used as the setting for the film *Doctor Dolittle*, there is nothing now to show for its brief life as a motion-picture capital. In fact, aside from the Marigot des Roseaux Hotel, a cluster of hillside cottages near the sea, there is nothing to mar the natural beauty of Marigot Bay at all. The hotel is located on the shore opposite the approach by road, and one summons a boatman by waving frantically. Although waits are long, he eventually shows up. The trip across the bay to the hotel takes less than five minutes, and drop-in visitors can sit at tables on a bamboo-thatched terrace and dine by lamplight or have cocktails. I asked the manager to show me some of the rooms of the hotel, and he led me up the hillside and opened the doors to two of the cottages: they were fairly primitive, but in a pleasant and quite livable way.

How can I describe the Anse Chastenet Hotel, near the little village of Soufrière, where I spent several days, since my judgment is clouded by the fact that I think it has become my favorite in the whole world and therefore all objectivity is beyond me? Well, for starters, it has no air conditioning and, indeed, not even window screens; moths and lesser insects took possession of my room after dark with an air of confidence too formidable for me to challenge. The hotel, a group of octagon-shaped cottages, is perched on the side of a cliff, and there is a sharp climb for those with sound wind of exactly 109 steps from the beach to the lowest of the buildings. Surrounding the hotel is nothing but jungle growth, the village is three miles away, and there is absolutely nothing to do. It has no snack bar, gift shop, or even a newsstand. What then is the reason for such devotion? Its remoteness, perhaps, its total informality, its friendliness and the indescribable beauty of its location. It was dark when I arrived by car, and that first night I was aware only of climbing up a steep hill behind a man carrying my suitcase (he was a guest the same as me, I discovered the next day to my embarrassment as I recall trying to force a tip on him) and stumbling in the dark along a narrow stone path beside what appeared to be a terrifying chasm. Two stout wooden doors opened, and I found myself in what turned out to be my quarters: a long, open verandah handsomely furnished with chaise longues; an immense bedroom with two sets of louvered doors opening on the verandah; a large bathroom; and a complete kitchen. But it was not until the next morning when I stepped sleepily out on the verandah that my heart leaped. The sun was bright, the sky was blue, and I could look down into the tops of palm trees that covered the slope of the cliff all the way to the sea. At one end of the porch the smaller of the two Pitons — massive volcanic peaks reaching up from the sea's edge — loomed close and slightly forbidding. A black sand beach, almost purple in the early morning light, could be seen far below. It was an exciting sight to wake up to. I pulled on a shirt and trousers and walked barefoot down the path to have breakfast in an outdoor dining room. There was a ripe mango, eggs and bacon, and excellent coffee. As I ate I heard the unmistakable thud of a tennis ball somewhere far below me, and while I couldn't see the court, I learned later there was a very good one a hundred yards or so behind the beach.

It is not that the area around Castries, in the north, has been deflowered by tourism, because St. Lucia in all respects is very much an unspoiled island, but the tempo of life around Soufrière appears to beat to a more authentically Caribbean rhythm. Soufrière was once the capital of St. Lucia, but it is now a sleepy little town, laid out in haphazard fashion around a central park that has the dubious distinction of having once contained the only guillotine ever to operate — on a businesslike basis — in the New World. The Soufrière Library, a block from the park, leans heavily toward the steamy fiction of Frank G. Slaughter, and offers its passing readers a few ragged copies of *The Listener*, *Punch*, and *Ms*.

A mile or so outside of town is the Still, which beyond doubt is the finest restaurant on the island and most likely one of the best in the Caribbean. Once a rum distillery, it has been converted into an impressively large dining room, and even now another stone building is going up beside the original one to provide more dining space. When I asked Michael du Bouley, the owner, where on earth did all of his customers come from, he smiled and shrugged his shoulders. "From Castries and from the hotels all over the island," he said. "Frequently Cunard cruise ships come in, and I suddenly find buses depositing 150 people here unexpectedly for lunch."

On the side of a mountain behind Soufrière is a remnant of the island's last active volcano. A fairly good road leads directly to the crater, and a guide there takes visitors on a carefully laid out tour, skirting the bubbling lakes of mud and sulfur. Although clouds of sulfuric steam sometimes belch out unexpectedly, the mud itself is not boiling; it is made to appear so by gases escaping from fissures in the earth's crust. The surface temperature in the hottest of the lakes is only 190 degrees Fahrenheit, but there is enough steam below the surface to convince a team of British drillers of the practicality of a geothermic power plant there that would be capable of generating enough electricity for the entire island. A remnant of the drilling project — a roaring jet of steam coming from a pipe beside the road — is still marveled at by visiting natives, who, curiously enough, find this man-made phenomenon far more fascinating a spectacle than that provided in the crater by nature.

At the foot of the mountain are the hot sulfur baths, which Louis XVI said made his soldiers feel like a million sous, ridding them of rheumatism, ulcers, and respiratory complaints. I went in the ancient stone bathhouse, hung my clothes on a peg in the dressing room, and descended the steps into the hottest water I have ever voluntarily entered. I stayed there for a half-hour, enjoying every second of it, and when I came out I felt a better man for having done it.

I can't say I was aware of any immediate improvement in my ulcer, and I didn't have rheumatism or any respiratory complaints to begin with, but it was a fine and satisfying experience and I can't recommend it too highly.

On my last night in St. Lucia I was invited to a cocktail party given by one of the two owners of the Anse Chastenet at his home a short distance from Soufrière. For my benefit, I suspect, he had rounded up a group of locals, including a handful of Americans who had settled there and a Dutch artist elegantly gowned in a long white dress. What made the lady artist stand out in my memory was not her beauty, which was considerable, nor her stylish dress, but the fact that she swept into the room unselfconsciously barefooted. I stood on the terrace outside the living room at twilight drinking rum and soda and watching the last light sweep across the peak of the Petit Piton. The night frogs had begun their symphony and, as on the night of my arrival, the air was soft and moist. I liked St. Lucia — its sleepy villages, its banana plantations, its pleasant people, its tiny coves and mountains and jungles, and cocoa and coffee beans drying in the bright sunlight. Right now it offers beauty and tranquillity and, in the currency of our times, that's a lot.

7

Dynamic and Latin:
The Mexican Paradox

THE extraordinary thing about Mexico City is that despite its rapid and uncontrolled growth — it now has eleven million inhabitants and within twenty-five years that figure is expected to grow to thirty million, making it the world's largest city — it still manages to retain its essential Mexican flavor, its exuberance, its Spanish-Indian graciousness, its Old World charm. But it is a vastly different city from what it was, say, ten years ago and visitors returning after a decade or more will not find the city of their memories. The torpor is gone; the fashionable shops in the Zona Rosa — the exclusive Pink Zone — close up during siesta time, but this is tradition only, and traditions have a way of dissembling once their need is filled. This city abandoned the mañana attitude years ago; it has been, for a long time, a cosmopolitan city, a metropolis in the best sense of the word. It possesses what is most likely the world's most exciting museum, its great artists — Rivera, Orozco, Tamayo, Siqueiros, Mérida, Guerrero, Martínez, Saldivar, Icaza, the list could seemingly go on forever — are revered and proudly exhibited, there are poets on every street corner, the Ballet Folklórico is an explosion of color and motion, and its music, from mariachi to symphony, is superb.

While the drowsy capital that Mexico City once was is gone forever, the city that has taken its place is not sure yet exactly what it is going to be. As the entire country shudders from the convulsion of overindustrialization and underdevelopment, Mexico City, being the nerve center of these vast changes, feels these developments the most. And how could any city go its old way when it is forced to absorb a half-million migrants a year?

One day recently I descended into Mexico City's new subway and, following the advice of a Mexican friend, I selected a time when there was no rush-hour congestion. It was a fine transit system, modern and efficient. The trains were fast and quiet, the stations attractive. A short time later I tried the subway when I had a need to cross the city quickly, and my timing was not so fortunate. I was swallowed up by a mass of homeward-bound workers, and I recoiled from a scene of chaos that rivaled New York at its worst. And yet, a couple of hours later, I walked down the Paseo de la Reforma, the city's proudest boulevard, and it reminded me of nothing so much as the Prado of Havana in the old days when that was one of the most gracious cities in the world. The street was quiet, a few lovers strolled in the twilight holding hands, an elderly shoeshine man sat in his own armchair beside his footrest, dozing contentedly as the lights came on across the city. This is the Mexico City of today, a city with a split personality: restless and dynamic one moment, lazy, Latin, and engaging the next.

One eats well in Mexico City, and one drinks good wine. There are countless good restaurants, and more than a few excellent ones. I was astonished by the beauty of the women, which comes from the lucky mixture of ancient Spanish and Indian blood: dark-haired, brown-eyed beauties with high cheekbones, olive skin, and full, sensuous mouths. In one smart restaurant one evening I glanced around and had the sensation that I was surrounded by a room full of women all resembling Dolores Del Rio. I could say nothing more flattering. Like the Spanish, the Mexicans have a strong puritan strain; dress is handsome but severe, manners are formal, the spirit of the city is one of dignity. The typical resident of Mexico City is Catholic, of course, but he is less gloomy about his religion, less ascetic, than the Spaniard or the Irishman.

Like Madrid, Mexico City eats later, stays up later, than any other city on the continent. One night, with a date, I arrived at the Focolare at eight o'clock for dinner. The captain looked at me as if he couldn't decide whether I was late for lunch or early for dinner. The restaurant was deserted. The better places — Calesa de Londres, Delmonico's, Normandy, Parador de José Luis — start coming alive around eleven o'clock, and very few private dinner parties start before ten. At most of the private parties I have attended in Mexico City, the most popular drink seemed to be Scotch, although the natives drink enormous amounts of beer during the daytime and there is every reason why they should since Mexican beers — most notably Carta Blanca and Bohemia — are among the best in the world. One day I drove outside the city to the caves and bodega of Pedro Domecq, and there sampled several first-rate Mexican wines, but wine doesn't seem to have a very strong hold on Mexican taste. Tequila is offered the visitor on all sides, especially the margarita cocktail, a mixture of tequila, Triple Sec, and lime juice, but, oddly enough, I don't believe I have ever seen a Mexican drink it. The

Mexican is torn between his traditional habits and the modern, international world that daily is intruding more and more into his consciousness. There are crowds in the smart cafés of the Zona Rosa, but in the narrow, ill-lit streets that intersect with Insurgentes Avenue there are also great numbers of people, mostly male, eating and drinking in tiny bars and restaurants that have lost none of their humble, Mexican simplicity. One enters a small café, noisy with the staccato chatter of Spanish, and the barman slides across the bar to you a foaming glass of *cerveza*. There is no attempt at elegance, this is a workmen's café. Food is served all day, and it is unpretentious Mexican food, cheaply prepared and cheaply priced. Fish, pork, and chicken form the backbone of the menu.

One morning I arose at four o'clock, and in the darkness took a cab to the Shrine of Guadalupe, about four miles from the city. It was raining steadily and the outskirts of the city, in the hour before dawn, were gloomy and depressing. I had dozed off, I think, and came awake quickly when the cab stopped. I asked the driver to wait for me, and I stepped out into the rain. The parking area chosen by my driver was poorly lit, if at all, and I stumbled about in puddles of muddy water until I reached the basilica, which has been vastly rebuilt and enlarged through the centuries. In the gray light of dawn, the huge cathedral was overwhelming and one could sense the strange drawing power that had made it a mecca for nearly four hundred years. Behind the basilica I could make out the dark shadow of the hill, upon which the Virgin of Guadalupe had appeared to a passing Indian, telling him to build a church for her on that very spot.

I assume that the basilica is never closed because at that early hour there were hundreds of people moving silently about, lighting candles, praying, wandering from the main cathedral into the small adjoining chambers. Mostly these seemed to be rural people, who had come seeking cures, or were offering prayers of gratitude for good fortune, or merely rededicating themselves to their faith at a sacred and holy site. In one small room, lit only by the flicker of votive candles, an ancient Indian supported by a crudely carved crutch stood in front of an altar, the creases in his face set in pain but his eyes expressing hope. It was a moving and impressive thing.

Up until a few years ago, when students became restive all over the world, the University of Mexico was a much-respected institution of higher learning, and it possessed the added distinction of being the oldest university on the American continent. Now it is a sad and dismal place, the campus littered with filth and the buildings splattered with political slogans. I was taken there one afternoon by a Mexican friend who had received his medical education there, and I could see that the visit pained him. "The radical students took over and destroyed the school," he said sadly. "And it got so big, so swollen with students, that the quality of instruction dropped to almost nothing. It has almost no standing as a university now. A person who wants to become a doctor now goes to Guadalajara."

Sunday in Chapultepec Park is a delight equaled nowhere else that I know of. This enormous wooded area in the heart of the city was once used by the Aztec emperors for their private pleasures but now it is the place where Mexicans of all economic levels can go to escape the heat and the crowded streets of the city and discover a little of the vanishing serenity of country life. I strolled through the park one Sunday morning and I don't think I have ever seen a public facility so thoroughly enjoyed. *Charros*, or

cowboys, filled the bridle paths, whole families were un-
packing picnic lunches on the grass, rowboats filled the
lagoon, children screamed with delight as they rode goat
carts, donkey carts, and the miniature train. And anybody
in Mexico City who has anything to sell must surely have
set up a stand under the giant ahuehuete trees that shade
the area. One didn't have to move twenty feet to buy a
balloon, cotton candy, T-shirt, souvenir, kite, magazine,
pennant, or an infinite variety of snacks, almost all of
which smelled delicious. Chapultepec Park (the word
means grasshopper hill) also contains a first-rate zoo, an
extensive botanical garden, several bandstands for outdoor
concerts, a variety of playgrounds, an amusement park
complete with roller coaster, and last, but certainly the
most important, the famous Museum of Anthropology and
History. It is my firm conviction that this is the most exciting museum in the entire world, and anything that is said
about it is likely to be an understatement.

I'm not sure how one describes the Museum of Anthropology and History. To list the facts — that it was opened
in 1964 and that it relates through the use of displays the
history of the Aztec, Mixtec, Zapotec, Toltec and Tarascan
cultures — is a little like saying that *My Fair Lady* is the
story of a girl getting remedial speech lessons. The essential
spirit of the place is missed. I can only say that the museum
is brilliantly designed, that it is a place of enormous excitement, and that even children find its displays imaginative
and alive. I suggest more than a single visit because such a
broad panorama cannot be fully absorbed in a short period
of time. However, there is a good restaurant in the museum
for those who want to make a day of it, and plenty of
chairs and benches for rest. On my last visit there I discovered, in a vitrine filled with books and reproductions of

ceramic objects for sale, two dancing dogs, relics of the Classical Period. The original object had been unearthed at Colima, and from it some excellent reproductions had been made. I bought a reproduction of the dogs for the absurdly low price of nineteen dollars, and I find them so engaging that I don't think I can ever be induced to part with them.

South of Mexico City, perhaps fifteen kilometers or more, are the pyramids of Teotihuacán, which stand guard over the ruins of an ancient city that was old when the Aztecs first arrived in the Valley of Mexico. I went to the pyramids early one morning with a hamper, thinking to have lunch later in the day on top of the Pyramid of the Sun. Having forgone breakfast for an early start, I grew hungry as we threaded our way through the outskirts of the city, and I asked the driver to take me first to the village nearest the pyramids. I've forgotten the name of the village and I'm sorry because it was a pleasant place and I was treated with kindness by the people there. Although the time was barely seven o'clock, I found the village bakery open and filled with customers buying loaves of bread and pastries still warm from the oven. I selected a loaf of bread for lunch and a couple of sweet rolls for breakfast and, guided by the baker's wife, made my way across the dirt road to a café that had just thrown open its doors. The owner explained it would take a few minutes to make fresh coffee and, meanwhile, I was to enjoy the music at his expense. He slipped a coin in the slot of a jukebox, and the sound of a mariachi band emerged at a volume that threatened to shatter my eardrums. I was helpless to object for fear of offending the proprietor, so I ate one of the sweet rolls and did my best to ignore the music blasting out of the machine beside me. The record ended and the coffee arrived simultaneously. The coffee was good and the silence was better.

I wandered through the excavated ruins of the city, and around noon I started climbing to the top of the Pyramid of the Sun. Unlike the Egyptian pyramids, those of Teotihuacán have steps — frightfully steep but steps nevertheless — leading from the ground to the summit. It's best to slog along and not look back, I discovered. It was a stiff climb, but not too exhausting, and once at the top the view was remarkable. A short distance away was the Pyramid of the Moon, somewhat smaller than that of the Sun on which I stood, and between the two were the many altars that marked the Street of the Dead. I had lunch seated on a large slab of stone, alone except for two Japanese tourists who arrived, took a few photographs from the summit, and departed.

I have said nothing of Xochimilco, the famous "floating gardens" that are located fifteen miles from the city, largely because the spot is such a favorite of tourists that it has lost whatever character it once had and now is more theater than anything else. Much more to my liking is Cuernavaca, a small city about an hour and a half away, a city of flowers, gentle temperature, and sunshine.

I must say a word about the Zócalo, the big square in the center of Mexico City, for three reasons of equal importance. The first, of course, is that the Cathedral, thought to be the second in size only to St. Peter's in Rome, is located there and must be visited. Second, on a street bordering the Zócalo can be found the National Pawnshop, a building containing an incredible collection of unclaimed jewelry and other items, all of which are for sale and some at rather startling prices. (Mexicans, being a sentimental people, refer to the building as the Monte de Piedad or the "hill of pity.") The third reason for visiting the Zócalo is that around the corner from the Monte de Piedad is the Grand Hotel, a small, relatively inexpensive place that is filled with such grace and charm that one is not likely to forget it. Once a department store, it demonstrates what can result when good taste and imagination are brought to bear on a restoration.

There is reason to worry about the Mexico City of the future. Already it is too big, the seams are beginning to give, the stress is showing. The Mexicans themselves are worried; they know their city and they like it the way it is. They feel about it as they feel for their family or their close friends; if they neglect it, it is the neglect of unawareness. Their hand is still stretched in welcome to the visitor to their city, whether the visitor seeks the glamour of the tall hotels on the Paseo de la Reforma or the idleness of the little squares. Both are there. And the native of Mexico City genuinely hopes it will remain that way.

8

Landmarks

Meanwhile Hitler had finished lunch, and his guests had been dismissed. For a time he remained behind; then he emerged from his suite, accompanied by Eva Braun, and another farewell ceremony took place. Bormann and Goebbels were there. . . . Frau Goebbels was not present. Unnerved by the approaching death of her children, she remained all day in her own room. Hitler and Eva Braun shook hands with them all, and then returned to their suite. The others were dismissed, all but the high priests and those few others whose services would be necessary. These waited in the passage. A single shot was heard. After an interval they entered the suite. Hitler was lying on the sofa which was soaked with blood. He had shot himself through the mouth. Eva Braun was also on the sofa, also dead. A revolver was by her side but she had not used it; she had swallowed poison. The time was half-past three.

— The Last Days of Hitler
by H. R. Trevor-Roper

It was a gloomy day, heavily overcast and uncomfortably raw, when I offered my passport to an East German border guard at Checkpoint Charlie. It disappeared on an assembly belt, and I passed on into another room where, after I had filled out a few forms and bought the required number of East German marks, my name was eventually called and my passport restored. I stepped out on Friedrichstrasse, in East Berlin, and crossed the street to a travel agency. I had been in East Berlin the day before, visiting the Soviet War Memorial, and I had met an extremely congenial guide who had told me I could find him just beyond the border station and that he would help me in any way that he could. He was seated at a desk when I opened the door, but he arose quickly and offered me his hand. He seemed genuinely pleased to see me.

I told him very simply that I possessed a street map of East Berlin and I would be greatly obliged if he would indicate on it the site of Hitler's bunker, or the approximate site of it, since I would like to visit it. I had been told it was within walking distance of Checkpoint Charlie.

"There's nothing there to see," he said, taking his seat. "Absolutely nothing. The whole area was bombed out, and the site of the Reichschancellery was bulldozed by the Soviets. There's only an open space, with a small mound of rubble where the bunker was."

I said I had been told all that in West Berlin, but nevertheless I wanted to see it. Would he kindly indicate on my map where the Reichschancellery had stood? He took the map, spread it flat on his desk, and studied it a moment. "Everything in that area is approximate," he said, taking a pencil from the desk. "It's mostly an open field and there's not much to go by. All of the big stones were hauled off to be used in the Soviet War Memorial. But it's roughly in this area" — he made a loop on the map with the pencil — "and it's no more than a fifteen-minute walk from here. But if you find it, I think you will be disappointed." I took back the map, shook hands again, and left.

At Leipzigerstrasse there was a bar on the corner, and I went in and asked for a beer. The bartender was reading a comic book called *Dennis der Menace*. I paid for the beer and took it to a table near a window. The view was dismal and dispiriting: a scattering of low, gray stone buildings set apart by bombed-out areas in which junk had been thrown to grow old with the rubble. Yellow buses ran along Leipzigerstrasse carrying workmen; an elderly woman seated on a bench had taken off her shoes, and when she saw a bus approaching she hurriedly put them on again. The bus stopped, its brakes squeaking loudly. Across the street was a huge pile of construction waste, on top of which was a sign saying, *"Durchgang verboten."* Both the waste and the sign had been there a long time. It began to rain softly.

When I came out of the bar I followed the map a couple of blocks to Otto-Grotewohlstrasse. Here was an apartment building of ancient stone, gutted on one side but with clean white curtains hanging at the windows of the restored wing. I wondered what it was like to live in a building, part of which had been destroyed thirty years ago, but so much of East Berlin was made up of the shells of buildings. It was commonplace to come upon a block of roofless buildings, or a stairway leading to nowhere, or gaping, empty windows. I had been told in West Berlin that 85 percent of this entire area had been destroyed, and indeed it had. The street I was on, in the next block, became Thälmannplatz, and suddenly I was aware of an immense bare field enclosed by a high wire fence. On the other side of the field ran the Berlin Wall, and in the center, perhaps fifty yards from where I was standing, was a small mound about fifteen feet high containing earth and rubble. This was it.

Under this mound was Hitler's bunker, its corridors and rooms a sealed tomb. It was here, on April 30, 1945, that the Third Reich — which Hitler had proudly proclaimed would last a thousand years — had come to a crashing, fiery end. This was the end of the straight-armed Nazi salute, the goose-stepping masses of storm troopers, the aggression against more than half of Europe, the seeming endless panzer divisions, the Luftwaffe, the bestiality of Buchenwald and Auschwitz, the gauleiters, the Brown Shirts, the secret police and all of the other terrible and dreary elements of the Nazi apparatus.

I followed the fence until I came as close to the mound as I could get. The field was grown up in weeds and there were three large signs warning people to keep away. The mound itself was mostly earth, but large stones could be seen protruding from it. The Reichschancellery had been Hitler's pride, a vast building of marble and glass, its great halls richly hung with paintings and lighted by gleaming candelabra. It was to this handsome building that he moved his military headquarters, and when it was bombed, he ordered the bunker built in the garden fifty feet below ground. This pathetic pile of rubble was all that remained.

Standing there in the gentle rain of an autumn day, nearly thirty years later, it was difficult to imagine the drama that had acted itself out on that stage in the final days of Hitler's life: the bombs, the frantic activity, the coming and going of couriers, the generals and admirals bringing Hitler news of accumulating disaster, the staff cars and motorcycles roaring in and out, the steady bombardment, the flaming buildings and the clouds of smoke. Now it was deathly quiet, and only weeds, nourished by the ashes of Adolf Hitler, grew in the field. I could see an armed guard in a tower of the Berlin Wall, and around the corner came a workman wearing a red hard hat. There were no other signs of life.

I asked the workman if this had been the Reichschancellery, and he looked puzzled. Then he said, "Ja, ja," and moved on. He was old enough to have been in Berlin at the time. Halfway down the street, he looked back at me curiously.

The bunker itself, I had read, had been built on two levels. On the upper level were the servants' quarters and the kitchen, and perhaps an office or two, all built on either side of a central passage. At the end of the passage was the stairwell to a larger bunker on the lower level, and here were located the private quarters of the Fuehrer. In bulldozing the site, the Soviets had wanted to guarantee that nothing was left upon which the myth and legend of Hitler might feed.

I walked to the end of the street, and there the fence turned at right angles and moved in the direction of the Wall. I was very close now to a tower and to the line of standards at the top of which were floodlights. Beside the street, fitting snugly into a corner at the end of the Reichschancellery fence, was a tiny children's playground. It was forlornly empty, and a sign rising from a sandbox said, "*geschlossen.*" From a construction site behind me came the staccato sound of a jackhammer, and it sounded so like a machine gun that my impulse was to throw myself on the ground. I looked once more at the mound, then turned and walked back to Checkpoint Charlie.

It was raining very hard when I came out of the passport

control station in West Berlin, and I was glad to get a taxicab back to Kurfürstendamm.

Hamlet's Castle

I'VE always taken a poacher's rather than a gamekeeper's view of the boundaries of travel, and when I arrived at Helsingor one snowy day and found Elsinore Castle closed for the winter I went straight for the custodian's cottage. It was bitterly cold and it had snowed heavily ever since I boarded the train in Copenhagen. When I came out of the Helsingor station, cruel gusts of wind were blowing in from the Oresund, the narrow sound that separates Denmark from Sweden, and I wasted not a second in getting in a taxicab. Over the turned-up collar of my overcoat, I caught a glimpse of what I took to be the towers of the castle not far from the harbor. When I told the driver my destination, he turned around for a closer look at me.

"Elsinore Castle?" he asked. It was as though I had asked him to drive me to Moscow.

"Elsinore Castle," I replied, pulling my overcoat around me. He studied me for a moment, offering me every opportunity to pull the punch line of what was obviously a joke. "The castle is closed," he said. "It isn't heated. Nobody goes there in the winter."

I said that I had come from New York and, one way or another, I was intent on going through the castle. I asked for suggestions.

The driver was still studying ways to dismiss this madness, not advance it. "It will be dark very early today," he said. "The castle is not lighted. Even if you got in there, you would not be able to stay long." I shook my head firmly. "I must go to the castle," I said.

He started the cab. "I will take you to the custodian," he

said. "But I don't think he will be very glad to see you." The cab skirted the harbor, moved through several very narrow streets, and came to a stop in a large open area. In front of us was a moat, on which some black swans were swimming, and across it loomed the castle. It was snowing hard when I stepped from the cab, and the castle looked gray, quiet and deserted.

The cabdriver motioned toward a low building that looked as if it had once been a stable. "You'll find the custodian there," he said. "Just knock on the door. He will probably have you committed to a madhouse." I paid the driver, and he paused. "Perhaps I'd better wait," he said. I shook my head. "Thank you," I said, "but it's not necessary. I'm going in the castle."

"As you wish," he said pleasantly. "But don't expect the custodian to be pleased to see you."

He wasn't. He opened the door and stood well out of the reach of the snow, staring at me in disbelief. He was stocky, his face was very red, and he was wearing only long underwear. Not knowing who had rung the bell, he was wearing his official cap. He repeated what the cab-driver had said and added a few new objections of his own. It was absolutely impossible to visit the castle. When I persisted, he motioned for me to come in and closed the door behind me.

"I have an idea," he said, his face breaking into a jovial smile. "You want to know about the castle? All right, we'll go to a small bar that is less than a five-minute walk, and I'll tell you all you want to know about it. How's that?" He went into the next room and appeared a few minutes later, stuffing a shirt into his trousers. "That will be a bit more comfortable than walking around in the cold castle, won't it?"

I said no it wouldn't. I was determined to go through the castle, I said, and if he didn't want to accompany me, would he let me go through alone? He shrugged in a gesture of surrender. "I must lock you up there," he said. "The castle door can't stay open." I said that was satisfactory with me. He pulled on a coat, wrapped a muffler around his neck, adjusted his official cap at the proper angle, and opened the door. "This is the first time I've ever had such a request," he said, as we stepped out into the snow. "You Americans are insane."

Once outside his manner became instantly professional. "The real name of the castle is Kronborg," he said. I was walking fast and he was having a little trouble keeping the pace. "It was built by King Frederik II in 1574. On the night of September 25, 1629, the castle was devastated by a terrible fire."

I interrupted to say that I felt a certain resistance to specific dates and that I'd be obliged if he would just round things off to the proper century. "Incidentally," I asked, "is there any evidence that Shakespeare ever visited this castle?"

He stopped abruptly, seized my arm and turned me toward the moat. "No," he said, "but there's one bit of evidence that is very mysterious, very tantalizing. Look in the moat at the plants that grow in the cracks and between the rocks. They're dead now, but in the summer they are a green fern and they grow there and nowhere else in Denmark. The plant is called *ruta murøta* here, and Shakespeare includes it as one of the flowers in Ophelia's bouquet. Now, how did Shakespeare know about that plant if he was never here?" The custodian looked triumphant. I agreed that it was, indeed, an engaging fact, and was properly distressed when I reread the play later and found nothing in Ophelia's bouquet that could be identified with the fern.

I was already cold when we reached the great door to the castle, and I was beginning to have doubts about the wisdom of my decision. The key turned in the lock, and with both hands he pulled the huge door open. Shakespeare's stage settings and directions were sparse, often consisting of no more than "A platform before the castle" or "Exit Ghost." But the play had converted the castle into a haunted place in my imagination, and I was having difficulty seeing it as anything but sinister. The custodian pointed out to me the S-shaped entrance, which prevents weapons from being fired directly into the castle, and the plaque to Shakespeare that had been set into the wall, and he explained that we had just entered through what was called the Dark Gate. The name was a triumph of accuracy.

We stood there in the entrance a few minutes. "People ask me which was Hamlet's room," he said, "or where was Hamlet's father when the uncle poured poison in his ear, or where in the castle did Hamlet and Laertes fight the duel. I wish I could tell them because they want to believe it so badly. You know the play used to be presented in the courtyard each summer. A stage was built at the east end, and folding chairs were set up for the audience. Once Richard Burton and Claire Bloom played the leading roles here."

I asked why the productions had been stopped.

"Rain," the custodian said glumly. "Too many times it was rained out."

We both fell silent. "Well," he said, "I shouldn't hold you up. It will get dark early today. I must lock the door. What time shall I come for you?"

"Give me three hours," I said, in a rush of bravado.

He looked at me in astonishment. "You will freeze to death in three hours," he said. "Two at the most."

"Two and a half," I countered. He shrugged. "Just as you wish," he said. He disappeared around the S curve, and I heard the heavy door slam shut and the key turn. I was alone.

Although the castle was cold, it was a relief to be out of the wind, and I found that if I walked rapidly and climbed stairs briskly the cold became endurable. It had been a long time since anyone had climbed up to the King's Tower, because cobwebs were everywhere. I brushed the dust from the leaded glass window, and gazed out at one of the bleakest landscapes I have ever seen. The snow had turned to rain, and smokestacks on the Swedish side of the sound could be dimly seen through the mist. The castle stands on an exposed point of land with the sea on three sides of it, and over the howling of the wind I could occasionally hear the ghostly foghorn of a ship. The clouds were low and heavy, and although it was now early afternoon, darkness wasn't far off.

The only room in the castle that reflected any cheer was the Queen's Chamber, and to say that it was cheerful requires enormous generosity. But it was lighter than most of the rooms, its fireplace was magnificent, it had a modest but graceful candelabrum, and its walls were covered in gilt leather. On the ceiling were seventeenth-century paintings representing Apollo, Diana, Dawn, Night and Neptune. The room was spare but regal, and reinforced my belief that despite the trappings of royalty, life in a castle was hideously uncomfortable and cheerless.

I had been told that the Great Hall, on the third floor, was the largest in all of northern Europe, and I haven't the slightest doubt that this is true. It is nearly 250 feet long and when occupied by one person seems much larger than it is. The ceilings were beamed, and the hall contained no furniture except a few chairs against the walls. As I walked the length of the Great Hall to inspect the paintings and tapestries, my footsteps seemed to echo throughout the entire castle. The hall possessed the stale odor of a place long closed, and whenever I paused, and the sound of my footsteps died away, it was deathly quiet. I was glad to move on.

Darkness was arriving fast when I made my way back to the Dark Gate. I had been in the castle only two hours, but the custodian was waiting for me. He was carrying a book which he handed to me. "This is the history of Kronborg," he said. "Now you should go to a hotel or restaurant and have some aquavit to warm you up." He had a cab waiting for me.

The driver suggested the Hotel Marienlyst, and we started off. It was snowing again and I realized that I was painfully cold. The dining room of the Marienlyst was spacious, well lighted and cheerful, and after my second aquavit I detected warmth returning to my hands and feet. It was pleasant sitting there, and I began to leaf idly through the book the custodian had given me — a handsome, well-illustrated volume. The last paragraph suddenly caught my eye. It said:

"In the mind of the English-speaking visitors Kronborg is closely connected with Shakespeare's Hamlet. All this is legend. We only know for sure that the Earl of Leicester's players were in Elsinore in 1586–87."

Man is the supreme illusionary; he likes nothing better than to believe his own fairy tales. In Verona, guides tell you with perfect composure where Romeo and Juliet lived, and in Hamelin, tourists with young hearts and open minds are shown the Pied Piper's house. But the most firmly established and persistent legend in the whole arcanum of make-believe is that Hamlet walked the battlements of Elsinore Castle. Hamlet didn't, but I did.

Berggasse 19

A LITTLE of the faded romance that clings to Vienna is enough. It's not as though the city isn't pleasant and certainly it's lovely to look at, but rather it is a bit *too* baroque and I found that I could be overwhelmed by chocolate, opera, pastry, boys' choirs and horses. I wandered through Schoenbrunn Castle by the hour, marveling at the beauty of the building and the atrocious taste of the Hapsburgs who had inhabited it; I visited — I'm sure — all thirty of the buildings in which Beethoven had lived and from which he had been ejected for nonpayment of rent, or for making too much noise, or for just being ornery; I climbed up the stairs of an inner court and spent the better part of a morning in Figarohaus, where Mozart had composed *The Marriage of Figaro* and where he had been visited by Beethoven and Haydn; I thrilled to the splendor of the Spanish Riding School and I spent a memorable Sunday morning listening to the Vienna Boys Choir and wondering how much longer the women's liberation leaders were going to permit it to continue. But my most rewarding experience in Vienna, for some odd reason, came very late one foggy night when I was returning from Grinzing.

In case there is anyone left who doesn't know it, Grinzing is a small suburb of Vienna in which are located a number of wine gardens and small cafés that offer their patrons not only reasonably robust food but also vast quantities of *heuriger*, or young wine of the latest vintage. A friend had taken me to a café there called the Grinzinger Wine Cask, and we had not only eaten heartily but we had drunk an immoderate amount of *heuriger*. I recall that we had also sung quite a bit, making up in volume what we lacked in tonal fidelity. Altogether the evening had been rich in gemütlichkeit and, perhaps, overly rich in *Schrammeln*. How does one describe *Schrammeln?* It is Viennese music as played by *Schrammeln* ensembles, taking its name from the brothers Johann and Josef Schrammel, who are credited with bringing Viennese music to a peak in the second half of the nineteenth century. Wherever the *Schrammeln* are playing, they tend to get rather noisy as the evening wears on and this was most certainly the case on the evening I am describing.

A heavy fog had descended upon Grinzing when we left the restaurant and found our way to my friend's car, and it seemed to get thicker as we approached the center of town. I was staying at a small hotel on Schottering, and my friend promised that despite the fog he would have no trouble in locating it. We drove slowly down Vahringer, past Thurngasse, and then he said, peering intently through the windshield, that Berggassestrasse should be next. The word struck a chord in my mind like a bell. *Berg* meant hill and *gasse* was a small street — smaller than a *strasse* — but, more important, I remembered that Sigmund Freud had lived and practiced psychoanalysis at an address on Berggasse. I directed my friend to stop, and explained that I had drunk too much wine and would like to walk the rest of the way to my hotel in the hope of clearing my head. "But your hotel is half a dozen blocks away," he protested, "and in this fog —"

I told him not to worry, and opened the door. We shook hands, he changed gears, and was gone. The fog closed in on me; I could scarcely see across the street. I glanced at my wristwatch, and saw that it was either one o'clock or two o'clock, I couldn't tell which, although I held the watch within a few inches of my eyes and squinted. It was quiet, and I saw no one. Isolation in the country is perfectly natural; in the middle of a city it is somehow unsettling.

I walked slowly down the hill, and a green neon sign suddenly broke though the mist. It was the Café Lichtenstein, and apparently it was still open. In a window was an illuminated sign that said STOCK and another that said *Trink Coca-Cola*. I crossed the street diagonally, drawn by a lighted shop window, and saw that it was a wig shop. The street was wet from the mist and occasionally drops of water fell from wires and signs overhead. The garish green light of the Café Lichtenstein faded into a shapeless image behind me, and I was again walking on a deserted and lifeless street.

And abruptly I came upon it. Berggasse 19 was a solid building whose stone façade had been patched many times with concrete that stubbornly refused to age. One entered it through a large glass and metal door, and beside the door was a modest metal sign which read: SIGMUND FREUD, GESELLSCHAFT, MEZZANIN. Another sign, smaller and more recent, read: *In diesem haus lebte und wirkte Professor Sigmund Freud 1891–1938.*

It was here, on this quiet street and in this building that was no different from thousands like it in Brussels or Rotterdam or Berlin or Zurich, that Dr. Freud had received his patients, listened intently to their secrets, and patiently developed the psychoanalytical theories that would help provide the world with a new medical science. Standing there in the mist, I wondered how many of the patients that had passed through that door had realized that the bearded professor they would meet in the mezzanine consulting room was, even then, becoming a major figure in medical history. And then Hitler had overrun Austria and as the virus of anti-Semitism began to poison the bloodstream of Vienna, Dr. Freud had slipped from that building and fled.

I was cold; the dampness had penetrated my coat. In the distance, I heard a streetcar screech as its wheels ground around a curve. The fog had not lessened, and I turned and started back up the hill. When I reached the Café Lichten-stein, the green light had been turned off and the restaurant was closed. I walked through the silent streets of Vienna to my hotel.

9

The Girl from Ipanema

COLLECTORS of moonbeams should reconsider the myth of the Girl from Ipanema and with a somewhat modified rapture. Instead of being tall and tan and young and lovely, she's much more likely to be short and chunky, very hot-eyed, not very pretty, and a great deal darker than tan. She giggles a lot, speaks only Portuguese, and she eats almost continuously. Worse still, Ipanema Beach is polluted. I make this melancholy deposition having left the beach about ten minutes ago in order to set down my impressions while they are still fresh and to rearrange what few illusions I have left.

Ipanema Beach is one of four beaches in Rio de Janeiro, and one that was totally eclipsed by the more famous Copacabana Beach until Antonio Carlos Jobim's song cataloguing the charms of "The Girl from Ipanema" became popular in 1963. The two beaches come together at one point, and for the life of me I don't see how one tells which is which but, I am told, fierce loyalties exist and the Ipanema crowd wouldn't be caught dead on Copacabana and, presumably, vice versa. But on a hot day both beaches are crowded, there are probably five hundred different soccer games going on simultaneously on both of them, and there is an endlessly fascinating parade of barefooted salesmen offering fresh pineapple, coconuts, jewelry, watches, straw mats, kites, soft drinks, and ice cream on a stick. The latter is pretty good and I place my seal of approval whole-heartedly on the Kibon; the Yopa — I found — was of a lesser grade. Where popsicles are concerned, I do not casually lower my standards.

I arrived at Ipanema Beach about ten-thirty in the morning, just as a light fog began drifting out over the ocean and the sun started to penetrate the haze. The beach was already crowded, and there were two games of volleyball being played so close together that I would swear the players occasionally intermingled. The ritual of arriving and settling on the beach is coldly precise and any departure from established custom is not to be considered. The girls arrive, mostly in pairs, each wearing a towel around her waist to cover what is perhaps the skimpiest swim suit ever worn in public. It is called a tonga, and just the thought of describing it brings color to my cheeks. A rolled-up mat is tucked under the arm, and each girl carries a beach bag. Approved procedure then calls for digging a hole, always with the foot, and using the excavated sand as a backrest. Sometimes one can find a hole, or a pair of holes, already dug and abandoned for some reason, but seldom do abandoned holes face the sun. Once the hips are lowered into the hole, the person remains there rotating slightly with the sun. This is the rotisserie principle in its simplest form. Men promenade, eyeing the girls, but the latter seldom move, since to do so would require the movement also of all possessions. Anything left in the sand for more than thirty seconds finds a new owner. In some places this is called stealing, but I gather it isn't considered so on Ipanema Beach.

I would like to report briefly on the subject of girl-staring at Ipanema, since this, aside from soccer, is the principal activity and one that is obviously popular with both sexes. The men march, prowl, or cruise — I'm not sure which is the most precise word — and the girls remain seated in the sand, but when a man eyes a girl who attracts him it appears acceptable custom that he can stop in his tracks and stare at her for as long as he wishes. The glances are thorough and wide-ranging. If the girl likes the attention, she will smile; if not, her admirer will be ignored. It seems that little more than this is involved in the game, although it stands to reason that the gap is occasionally bridged by a more personal contact. However, Brazilians, as a rule, seldom touch in public and demonstrations of affection are not thought well of.

A short man carrying two enormous aluminum cylinders strapped to his back struggled through the sand, and I could hear ice rattling in the cylinders. I gestured to him and he came over, lowered one cylinder and poured me a cup of an herb tea called mate. It cost twenty cents and was much too heavily sugared for my taste; I poured most of it in the sand. The sun was getting hot now, and I got up, put on my pants and shirt, and walked across Avenida Atlântica and down Rua Montenegro a few blocks. There was a small café on the corner, and I sat at a table on the sidewalk and ordered a Coca-Cola and a Sandwich Americano. The latter turned out to contain melted cheese, ham, and a fried egg. The waiter, recognizing me as a foreigner, asked, in tortured English, how I liked Rio. I said fine. It was hot and the traffic was heavy. A passing dog lifted its leg against the table and the waiter snapped a napkin at it. The dog slunk away, unfulfilled. When the check came, there were two items charged that I hadn't ordered. When I asked the waiter what they were, his English suddenly vanished. I let it pass, and took the sum out of his tip. If he wanted it, he could collect from management. He knew the ways.

Back at the beach I found the haze had returned and the sun was now a red disk in the sky. My hole had been taken by a couple of young girls in tongas who had modified it somewhat and changed its orientation. I had to admit that the new tenants had improved things. I dug a new hole and was careful to make it neater. Sometime later in the afternoon, a sound truck moved down the Avenida Atlântica from the direction of Leblon Beach, blaring out a samba that could have been heard several miles at sea. The entire beach suddenly broke into a frenzy of dancing and it was at that moment that I learned that dancing is a reflex to Brazilians. Let a Brazilian girl hear three continuous notes of music and she abandons whatever she is doing and slips into motion; I gather the urge is greater than her ability to contain it. Music means dancing to a Brazilian, man or woman, and time and circumstance have no importance. I once saw a nurse, waiting on a street corner for a bus, break into a samba when an automobile went by with its radio playing loud. In a moment the car was gone, the girl in the white uniform shuffled a few more steps, and then straightened up and resumed her wait for the bus. It was as natural as though it had started to rain and she had raised her umbrella until the shower passed.

For those who imagine Ipanema Beach to be a white strand bordered with palm trees, I must bear unpleasant news. The beach is remarkably clean of trash, which I don't understand because the only litter receptacles are found beside the Avenida Atlântica, but it is not white and I counted only six scraggly palm trees along the entire esplanade. Ipanema has its own mosaic design in the sidewalk beside Avenida Atlântica, but it is not the flowing black and white curves that one associates with Copacabana. It is more of a geometrical design and not as pleasing to the eye as the famous waves of Copacabana. The city side of the Avenida, which curves around the entire arc of the Rio beachfront, is lined with modern apartment buildings, restaurants, and street cafés. Very few beach people, however, walk across the Avenida to eat in the restaurants, preferring instead to buy snacks from the beach vendors. The street cafés fill up around twilight, with most of the business done in tall glasses of Brahma, an inexpensive but excellent beer commonly called choppa for reasons I have never been able to learn. Later — around ten or eleven o'clock — the street girls appear, fairly pretty and well dressed for the most part, and they join hands with prospects and walk along the street with them, laughing and imploring. It seems a rather lively commerce, and one that appears to be accepted by the authorities and public alike as an innocent note in the symphony of a summer's evening.

Before I left Rio, I took a helicopter ride over the city and I shouted into the pilot's ear that I would like for him to take me over the beach area. From the air, as on the ground, it was impossible to distinguish one beach from another, but I could pinpoint Ipanema by identifying some of the buildings on the Avenida. It looked better from the air; distance added luster. And from that height, it was easy to imagine that all of those thousands of girls in tongas, leaning against their backrests of sand, were indeed tall and tan and young and lovely, just as the song says.

10

How to Murder Time
on the Orient Express

I HAD breakfast in the Munich station, and about a half-hour before the Orient Express was due to pull in I paid my check and walked down to the track. The train shed, like all European rail terminals, was immense and crowded; the cafés were filled, long queues formed at the ticket windows, and passengers and porters jostled each other in an erratic traffic flow that seemed to have no beginning and no end. Appropriately enough, the track designated for the Orient Express was Number 13, and when I arrived, there were already a half-dozen passengers standing around, guarding small mounds of luggage. None of them looked like spies or international criminals. No, that's not true. One did. He was short, clean-shaven, and bareheaded, and he appeared both nervous and furtive. Clearly he was involved in something sinister, and I had no doubt that he was wanted – perhaps frantically – by Interpol. Or he could have been a secret Russian agent on his way to Hungary. A girl was standing at his elbow, and I first thought that she was his companion, but she later moved to a kiosk to buy a magazine and when she rejoined the group she stood some distance away. I realized that proved nothing, but for some reason I decided she was clean. The other passengers were nondescript: two elderly ladies, a priest, and a young girl, obviously American, carrying a guidebook to Austria. She was sitting on her suitcase reading the guidebook with interest.

European trains are more often than not on time and at precisely 8:45 the train clattered into the shed. I glanced at my ticket which read: *Von München nach Wien, Wagen 266, Platz 55. Wagen 266*, it turned out, was in the middle of the train, and I found it without difficulty. *Platz 55* was in a compartment already inhabited by two stout women, who paused in their conversation only long enough to appraise me frankly and then resumed talking. I didn't recognize the language, which was no wonder in that collection of Europeans, Slavs, and Near Easterners. *Platz 55* was a window seat, and as I settled myself I gazed into the eyes of the occupant of *Platz 56*. It was the criminal.

Munich disappeared quickly as the train gathered speed, and soon we were moving through the rolling hills of Bavaria. From Munich to Vienna is almost a straight line east, but the train didn't go that way. It went south to Salzburg, then north to Linz, and from that point followed the Danube into Vienna. This leg of the Orient Express's journey takes six hours, and the way the train was speeding left little question that it would arrive on schedule. The compartment was hot and not knowing how to reduce the heat, I opened my collar and settled back in my seat, and in a few minutes I was dozing. The conversation of the two stout ladies made a pleasantly monotonous sound not unlike the clicking of the wheels on the roadbed. When I awoke, the train had stopped, and I was alone in the compartment. Seeing the criminal gone, I patted my inside pocket to make sure my passport was safe and reassured by the bulge, I straightened my tie, slid open the door to the compartment and moved into the corridor. It was cold there and when I got off the train it was colder still. We were in a small city surrounded by mountains, the peaks of which were covered with snow. "This is Salzburg," said a pleasant voice behind me, and I turned quickly to see the criminal. He took out a pack of cigarettes and offered me one. "It's unusual to see the sun on these mountains," he said. "Salzburg is a lovely city but it has terrible weather." I asked if he were Austrian and he shook his head. "No," he said, "I'm Hungarian. I'm on my way to Budapest, which is my home. And you are going to Vienna?" I started suspiciously. How did he know so positively? "I know you are going to Vienna," he said, "because very few people go to Budapest these days, and even fewer go to Bucharest. You will like Vienna. Everyone does."

A refreshment wagon pulled up and I bought a Swiss chocolate bar and a copy of *Paris-Match*. He declined my offer of candy with a gracious gesture. "We do not have such good dentists in Budapest as you do in New York," he said smiling, "so I eat very little chocolate." When we got back on the train the two stout ladies had gone, leaving the criminal and me alone in the compartment. He took off his coat, folded it neatly, smiled apologetically at me, and put his head back on the seat. In a few minutes he was asleep. The sun disappeared and a thick fog closed in on the train. I walked to the restaurant car where I had a croissant and coffee, and when I returned he was awake. He pointed out the window to a wide, sluggish gray river paralleling the tracks. "That's the Danube," he said. "We should be reaching Linz in a moment." As he spoke the train began to slow down.

I read a book from Linz to Vienna. The criminal took out some papers and fussed with them a bit, but his heart clearly wasn't in it, and he soon placed them back in his briefcase. He was gazing vacantly out of the window when the suburbs of Vienna came into view. I put on my trench coat and took my suitcase down from the rack. He stood up and held out a card. "Please call me if you ever get to Budapest," he said. "I'd be happy to show you the city. It is not so beautiful perhaps as it once was but it is a lovely place." I glanced at the card. It was in English and under his name was "Attorney-at-Law." We shook hands warmly, and I got off the train and walked down the long platform to the Vienna *Westbahnhof*. So far as excitement and intrigue were concerned, I might as well have ridden the Mozart Express. At the very least I could have stayed in bed two hours longer in Munich.

11

The Search for the Lemon Tree House

I DID not see what I would classify as a truly great beach until well on in life, and then my eyes fell upon Varadero Beach in Cuba. Old love affairs are not easily erased from the mind and heart, and while I do not want to dwell excessively upon a place that is regrettably not now accessible to the readers of this book, I can still close my eyes and re-create the wonder of Varadero: the long, white beach rimmed with sea grape and palm trees, the green water, the sun so hot on a February noon that it felt like a weight on the back, cold bottles of Hatuey *cerveza* served in a thatched-roof shack in the sand, and the persistent rumble of cha-cha-cha music coming from a dozen beach-front jukeboxes. The Cubans were (and I suspect still are) warm and friendly people. I never recall seeing a necktie there, and as many people — both native and visiting — wore shoes as didn't. The food was cheap and good; excellent, perhaps, if you fancy garlic.

People's notions of what constitutes an ideal beach vary widely, so I would like to set down my own preferences here and now, in order that those who disagree with me can disregard everything I'm going to say and move on promptly to the next chapter. First, I am happiest at what has come to be known as a "barefoot resort." An ideal barefoot resort for me would be something called the Lemon Tree House (I'm making this up, mind you), and it would be situated only a few yards from the beach, and it would have quarters for only six or eight people. There would be a wide verandah, and in the late afternoon the owner would wheel out a cart containing a variety of liquors, a big ice bucket, a lot of fresh limes, and a note pad on which the guests would list the drinks they had made for themselves. Guests would be largely ignored unless they wanted something, there would be comfortable chairs for reading, and at least one hammock for snoozing in the shade when the sun is at its hottest. Male guests would dress for dinner, and by that I mean put on a shirt; and the meal would be served on the verandah and eaten by the light of a few hurricane lamps. The village would be less than a quarter of a mile away, in the event some postprandial distraction were required. Days would begin whenever the guests wanted them to, and breakfast would be served out-of-doors, with lots of fresh fruit and good coffee, some lush tropical vegetation to look at, and a few butterflies exploring the bougainvillea. There would be a wreck in shallow water not far offshore, in case one decided later in the day to put on a mask and snorkel and swim leisurely out to watch the fish dart in and out of the portholes. One would sleep when sleepy and eat when hungry, and only these basic rules would apply. That's the kind of place I like.

The nearest thing to the Lemon Tree House that I ever encountered was on a small island off the coast of Malaysia in what I suppose would be called the Strait of Malacca. I had flown in from Bangkok early in the morning and, taking a taxi driver's advice, went directly from the airport to the Lone Pine Inn. This broke a long-standing principle of travel survival, because taxi drivers all over the world are corrupt and their opinions are worthless, but I had arisen early, I was tired and eager to get settled, and I figured that anyone else I asked for a recommendation would have exploited me as ruthlessly as I expected the taxi driver to do. I was pleased with the appearance of the Lone Pine Inn (what an incongruous name for a resort at a place called Batu Ferringhi!) — a group of neat bungalows scattered in a grove of casurina trees on a broad, deserted beach. My bungalow was clean and spacious, a refreshing breeze blew through the windows from the Strait of Malacca, and a boy arrived promptly with three bottles of mineral water on a tray, which he placed on a table and then left, with no thought, apparently, of a tip. I unpacked, put on a white shirt and shorts, and, barefooted, I stepped outside to the beach. I was pleased to see that preparations for breakfast were being made; several people were sitting at small tables in the sand, shaded by the casurina trees.

I took a table, placed my camera in the unoccupied chair, dug my feet into the sand, and looked around. The Lone Pine Inn would scarcely impress anyone looking for elegance; there were no more than fourteen or fifteen bungalows ringing a small office and kitchen. The bungalows were neat but undistinguished in any way, and, so far as I could see there were no tennis courts, putting greens, or anything else to amuse the guests. The beach was wide and unlittered, the water was green, the sun was warm and steadily advancing to hot, and that was it. The place possessed the polite air of apologetic decline, and I sensed there was a take-it-or-leave-it attitude on the part of the management. My impulse was to take it. I motioned to a waiter and asked for eggs, bacon, coffee and lemon pancakes.

I had finished my breakfast and was struggling to make a decision on the matter of a second cup of coffee when a small girl in a pink jumper, perhaps four or five years of age and remarkably pretty, wandered up to my table and gazed at me appraisingly. I have seldom been more carefully measured. It is a conviction of mine that children provide an emotional scaffolding that takes much of the stress of life if one permits it, so I spoke to her in English, trying to match but not mock her grave manner. I asked her name.

"Olga," she replied, but I didn't believe her and think she made it up on the spot. She didn't look like any Olga I had ever known. A large black mynah bird flew in softly and settled on the back of the other chair, casting its yellow eyes hungrily on my plate. It looked malevolent but I have been told this is not the case at all. The girl looked from me to the bird then turned her gaze back to me. It was as direct as though I were looking down a gun barrel.

"You had lemon pancakes," she said in an enviously accusing tone. I nodded. "I didn't," she said. "My father made me eat an egg." Her expression eliminated eggs from the face of the earth. There was half a pancake remaining on my plate and I pointed to it. "Would you like this piece of pancake?" I asked. The promptness of her reply betrayed the innocence of her approach. "Yes," she said, "and please put some more sugar on it. That's not enough." She gestured vaguely toward the plate.

She took the piece of pancake in her hand and, munching it with relish, walked down the beach. She had scarcely gone when a tall, swarthy man carrying a bag across his shoulder, came up. He stopped, brushed the bird aside, and pulled the chair out from the table. He shifted my camera from the chair to the table, and then very carefully placed the bag beside it. He sat down and gave me a smile that revealed the loss of a front tooth. "Do you know what's in the bag?" he asked.

"Yes, I do," I replied.

He didn't seem surprised. "What?" he asked.

"It's something you want to sell me and you're wasting your time. I don't want to buy anything."

He shook his head. "You're wrong," he said, smiling again. "I'm selling nothing. What I have in the bag is a cobra. I place the cobra around your neck and photograph you with your own camera." He pointed toward the camera. "Since it's very early in the morning and there isn't much business here on the beach, I will make you a special rate."

I couldn't conceal the uneasiness of my glance when I looked at the bag. Something inside it — the snake, no doubt — was moving. "You're out of your mind," I said, pushing my chair back from the table. "Take that bag away from here."

He smiled patiently. "The cobra is perfectly safe in the bag," he said, "and it would be safe around your neck. It's not a mean snake that strikes at everything." He picked up my camera and examined it. "You will have to show me how to operate this model. I don't believe I've ever used one."

I got to my feet. "Look," I said, "you're wasting your time. There is no possible way I would let you take that snake out of the bag, much less wrap it around me. I don't even want it on the table. Please take it away."

[97]

"But I haven't mentioned the price I would charge," the man protested. "When you hear how little it will cost you —"

My gesture cut him off in midsentence. "No photograph," I said firmly. "No cobra."

He arose, and picked the bag up from the table and swung it carelessly across his shoulder. "As you wish," he said agreeably, "but I am prepared to offer you a real bargain." He waved pleasantly and started away. Suddenly he stopped and turned around. "I can also put you in touch with a friend who sells batik very cheaply," he said. "If you will tell me the number of your cottage, I will have him call on you this afternoon and show you —"

I shook my head. "No batik," I said. "No batik. No cobra. No photograph. Nothing at all."

I asked the waiter for another cup of coffee, but before it arrived I had another visitor. It was a small Chinese boy, a few years older than the girl in the pink jumper, and he materialized suddenly beside me. Without invitation, he climbed into the chair recently vacated by the mynah bird and the cobra man, and gazed coolly across the table at me. "I can speak English," he said. I remarked that he did indeed. "Also," he went on, "I speak Malaysian and Chinese." There was a brief pause. "Want to hear me say something in Chinese?" I said that wasn't necessary because I believed him.

"Where do you live?" he asked.

"New York," I replied.

He thought that over for a moment while I added cream and sugar to my coffee. Suddenly his eyes flashed. "Would you like for me to go back to New York with you and be your son?"

I laughed. "That would be very nice," I said, "but I'm

sure your mother and father wouldn't care very much for it."

"I will go and ask them," he said with a great show of enthusiasm. "Don't go away because I'll be right back." He jumped off the chair and raced down the beach.

I guess I then took what one could reasonably consider the cowardly way out. Half expecting the Chinese boy to come trudging up the beach carrying a suitcase, I took my coffee and walked back to the bungalow. My visit to Batu Ferringhi had started on a high level of drama.

But it declined rapidly and the days that followed were dreamy, and fell away from me like leaves from a tree in autumn, changing only slightly from hour to hour, loosening, slipping, and — like the tree — I made no effort to hold them. I dozed in the afternoons, awakening to the shadow of a palm frond on the wall and speculating, by its distance from the ceiling, how long I had slept. Evenings offered a blessed nothingness; after dinner I could walk along the beach, my first alternative, or I could *not* walk along the beach, my second. If I was bored I was not aware of it, which is a rare and precious limbo to inhabit. I recall nights of moonlit triviality, but almost nothing that is specific and real. And as the days fell between my fingers like sand, I put off — I don't know how many times — my day of departure. Packing a bag and going to the airport seemed almost an obscene act.

I remember one thing. I was snorkeling one day, a hundred yards or more offshore, and what was idle disinterest in the occasional fish that swam out of the depths into my range of vision was suddenly shattered. I found myself surrounded by thousands of almost rectangular, vividly blue fish, whose bodies were outlined in luminous purple. They were indescribably beautiful and they swam on seemingly without end. I realized that I had somehow joined a vast school of the fish and that they were totally unconcerned with me as they moved on to wherever it was that they were heading. I tried momentarily to keep up with them, but they were moving at an incredible speed and changing course capriciously and unpredictably. I had never seen such fish; what they lacked in variety they made up for in sheer splendor. And, suddenly, they were gone, and I was alone in the water. I raised my head above water and pushed up the mask on my forehead, and gazed around me in search of some evidence that I had not imagined that surging column of motion and color, but the sea around me was calm and untroubled and, as always, its secrets were buried in its folds.

Several mornings I awoke early and, slipping on a shirt, trousers, and espadrilles, I walked along the road, smelling the jasmine that still hung in the early morning air and watching the shadows disappear as the sun rose over the small mountain that formed the spine of the island. One morning, as I walked along the road, I discovered a peculiar thing. I was suddenly conscious that I felt nothing, smelled nothing, and saw nothing; that I was completely numb. I listened attentively and I heard birds singing. I inhaled deeply and there was the odor of jasmine. I removed my shirt and I felt the cool brush of morning air against my skin. Living in New York, where there is too much noise, where the air is bad, and where one recoils from the touch of masses, did one unconsciously deaden one's senses? If so, once they were turned off it took a conscious effort to turn them on again. It was a disconcerting discovery.

Excitement stimulates and often exhausts. There was no excitement at Batu Ferringhi. I took a sail one day, in the Strait, and fell asleep before we returned. I took a taxi one morning into town, sat in the garden beside the sea at the ancient Eastern and Oriental Hotel and drank a gin and tonic, and raced back to the beach in near panic that I would miss my siesta. Once I went fishing with my young Chinese friend (who had adjusted quite comfortably to the knowledge that he could not go with me to New York) and we caught nothing. I was relieved because I get no pleasure watching a fish suffocate in the bottom of a boat, but Gan Swee Lai felt that our failure to catch something was in the nature of a personal defeat, and he was gloomy and silent as we walked back up the beach. At one end of the cove, on the left of my bungalow, were three large hills that one could call mountains by fooling around with the truth a little, and on top of the end one was a small light-house. I was told I could see Sumatra, across the Strait, from the lighthouse, but it was not true. I walked the two or three miles to the lighthouse one day, and I gazed in the direction of Sumatra but I could see nothing but blue-green water. Gan Swee Lai had accompanied me and we trudged back home along the beach, lazy and comfortable in the knowledge of our friendship, talking of meaningless things with the zest of veteran companions. On this, as on many other occasions, Gan Swee Lai did most of the talking and I muttered responses, or laughed at his whimsicalities, but when he grew silent I would assume the burden of conversation and talk to him of the city in which I lived. Then excitement would catch hold of him and he would pepper me with questions about the tall buildings and the big ships and the airplanes that flew into the airports in an endless stream, and the automobiles and the people and the zoos. More than anything else, the elevators strained his imagination; when I told him how one could be lifted fifty floors into the sky in less than a minute he would shake his head in disbelief and awe. Sometimes, in his excitement, he would lapse into Chinese and chatter on at a great rate before my laughter would make him remember that I understood not a word he was saying. Once he asked if I would like to come to his house and speak, and for a moment I was puzzled. Then I said, "You mean talk, not speak." He nodded. "Yes," he said. "Do you want to come and talk?" I said I would like that, but I never went. There was so much not to do at Batu Ferringhi that I didn't have time not to do it all.

I think it was Lawrence Durrell who said one could smell the whole of London in one pub or the whole of Paris on the crowded *terrasse* of a little student-quarter café, and so I felt the whole world of contentment on the warm sands of Batu Ferringhi. The days swam with color if without animation; the nights were soft and cool and still. I took generously of the ease, the silence, the contentment that was offered, I spent long hours reading, and I lay in the sand under the hot sun until my skin took on the color of cordovan leather. When I had slept so much that further sleep was impossible I would get up out of bed, put on trousers, and walk barefooted along the beach, letting the waves wash across my feet and sinking ankle-deep into the cool, wet sand, and I would study the stars, and wonder what the lives were like of the people in the tiny boats whose lights twinkled offshore. How cramped man's imagination is.

One day it rained, and Gan Swee Lai came and we walked in the rain together. It was not really to his liking; he didn't care to be wet but after the long succession of hot days I found it refreshing and I talked long and constantly about New York, hoping to divert him from his discomfort. The wind plastered our hair against our heads and made us squint to keep water from our eyes. When we got back to my bungalow, I summoned a waiter and asked for two cups of tea, and put a double portion of sugar in Gan Swee Lai's cup. This mollified him somewhat but did nothing to shake his conviction that I was a little crazy for wanting to walk in the rain.

I left Batu Ferringhi abruptly on a sultry afternoon. I had come in from the beach, showered, and was dressing for lunch when the knowledge came to me that it was time to go. I wanted to make no tedious preparations for departure, I wanted no unhappy farewell with Gan Swee Lai, and I had no taste for the sorrowful ritual of disengagement from a time and place of happiness. I paid my bill, got into a taxi, and directed the driver to take me to the airport at Penang. I knew it would be a mistake to look back, and I also knew — in my heart — that it would be a mistake ever to come back to Batu Ferringhi. There may be another Lemon Tree House in my life but it could only lie ahead. Meanwhile, I knew, Batu Ferringhi would recede in my memory through that curious process that obliterates all memories, both bright and sad, until only the shadowy outlines of those sunburnt days remained.

I wonder why it hasn't.

12

Finland, *Loyly*, Cloudberries and I

I WAS met at the lake steamer by Aarne, wearing white trousers and a T-shirt on the front of which was something printed in Finnish. Of all the languages of the world, Finnish, which is said to have some remote similarity to Hungarian, is the most incomprehensible to me. He greeted me warmly, took my overnight bag, and led me to an ancient automobile whose country of origin and identity had long ago been swallowed up by repairs and modifications. It started easily enough, and it took Aarne only a few minutes to maneuver it away from the dock area and on to a road that followed the shore of the lake. The lakes of eastern Finland, snug against the Russian frontier, are beautiful in a strange and wild sort of way; one is joined to another, like links in a chain, and they seem to push northward without end. The country surrounding the lakes is almost totally uninhabited and consists mainly of spruce and fir forests which grow to the edge of the water. There are few roads and fewer villages. My friend, whom I had seen a week before in Helsinki, had a country house somewhere in that wilderness. He told me it was twenty kilometers from the steamer; that's all I knew.

After the usual inquiries about my health, my work, and the journey from Helsinki were out of the way, Aarne got down to the subject of saunas. "We will get there in time for a sauna this afternoon and a swim in the lake," he said. "I told my wife to make the fire and have it ready by the time we arrive. Then we can have another tomorrow morning before you leave. If you wish, we can have a smoke sauna tomorrow." I shook my head. "I've read about smoke saunas," I said, "and it doesn't sound particularly appealing." Aarne laughed. "You know nothing about saunas in America," he said. "You speak of them as though they were great sexual adventures. Here they are not sexual at all. They are strictly family affairs."

I told him I had experienced saunas in America but that they were heated electrically, there were rugs and other refinements around, and I felt that we had extended ourselves so far in the direction of convenience that the historical and practical link had finally snapped. Now I wanted an authentic sauna. Aarne silently studied what I had said. "A sauna is a very simple thing," he said, "and the simpler it is, the more you are likely to enjoy it and the better it will be for you. Here in Finland, we think the sauna is of enormous physical benefit but that benefit depends entirely upon your ability to relax yourself while you are taking the heat. Relaxation is everything, and that's why we discourage conversation, singing, or whistling in the sauna. Shut out the outside world and its problems. All that talk about sweating out your poison and cleansing the blood is nonsense. Let's not claim virtues for the sauna that it doesn't possess."

The country house was set in a clearing in the spruce forest beside the lake. It was built of wood that had weathered to a silver color, and like so much in that coun-

try it was starkly simple. We left the car under the over-
hang of an outbuilding, and walked to the house. Aarne's
wife was a plump woman in her early forties, rosy-
cheeked, and without makeup. She wore a gray sweater
and a coarse, blue skirt. Her smile was pleasant and she
extended her hand in a friendly way. She spoke in Finnish
to Aarne, who laughed. "She says you came a long way to
take a sauna," he said. "She can't understand it, but she says
you are welcome anyway."

Aarne led me to the guest room, a sparsely furnished
room on the first floor that contained bunk beds, a hand-
woven rug, and a small table. There were hooks behind the
door upon which to hang clothes. I was told to meet Aarne
in the kitchen as soon as I was ready, and when I got there
Aarne's wife was slicing a large sausage on a wooden board.
"Have some," Arne said. "You're supposed to drink nothing alcoholic, not even beer, before the bath but sometimes
we eat a little sausage before the sauna and sometimes after
and sometimes not at all. But today is a special occasion.
We don't often have a guest from so far away." Aarne's
wife smiled as though she understood what her husband
was saying, and extended the board to me. I took a slice; it
was firmer than I expected but delicious. We sat around the
kitchen table, eating with our fingers. When the last piece
of sausage had disappeared, Aarne wiped his mouth with
the back of his hand, like a workingman in a Zola novel,
and stood up. "The sauna's ready," he said, "if you are."

We went out the kitchen door, walked around the
house, and started down a path toward the lake, Aarne
leading the way. The path skirted a marshy area, and when
we came again to the lake I could see a small pier ahead of
us leading out over the water. It rested on spruce logs that
had been driven into the lake bed, and like everything else

it had turned silver gray. On the land end of the pier stood two small buildings, one of which had a squat chimney from which a small swirl of smoke rose in the air. Aarne led me first to the other building, which turned out to be a small dressing room. There were towels on a table, a round, unpainted bench against one wall, and hooks for hanging clothes. Aarne sat on the bench and removed his shoes. "Forget all you've heard about the sauna," he said, "because I suspect a lot of it is nonsense. For example, it will not make you lose weight, because the weight loss is all moisture which you put back on immediately. It is pleasant, it cleanses you, it relaxes you and — if done right — it should refresh you. Almost all Finns take the sauna on Saturday, but don't ask me why because I don't know. Just a national habit, I suppose. Finnish athletes take saunas because they say it helps their physical condition, but I think it does so in an indirect way. The physical well-being of a person is improved by relaxation, especially mental relaxation. When you go in the sauna try not to take your problems with you. In fact, try to turn your mind off completely. That is the reason we talk very little in the sauna. The less mental activity there is, the more refreshed you will feel when you come out." He took off his clothes, hung them casually on a peg, and motioned for me to do the same. He held the door open and, naked, we walked across the small wooden bridge connecting the two buildings.

The inside of the sauna was plain. A small, round stove, topped with rocks, stood along the wall beside the door, and on the opposite wall were two long benches or shelves, one above the other but arranged like stairs. The floor, walls, and ceiling were birch planks. There was no thermometer and no window. The heat was fierce, and seemed to sear my lungs with each breath I took. Aarne spread out his towel on the top shelf, and indicated that I should do the same beneath him. When he closed the door, the only light that entered was through a small hole that had been cut into the wall near the stove and which, I suppose, furnished oxygen for the fire. The boards of my shelf were hot to the touch, but I laid the towel out full length and stretched out on it.

"How hot is it in here now?" I asked. Aarne replied that it was approximately 170 to 180 degrees Fahrenheit. "Forget about things like that," he advised. "Lie down, relax, and enjoy it. A sauna can be pleasant at only 140 Fahrenheit, but I prefer it much higher. I also recommend that you lie down because in that position the heat distribution is equal all over your body. Up here on the higher shelf, I have about five degrees higher temperature than you do. If you don't believe it, stand up." I told him I believed him, and we lapsed into silence. I began to perspire, a little at first and soon I could see my skin glisten in the semi-darkness.

A short time later Aarne climbed down from his shelf and opened the door. I almost welcomed the cool air that rushed in. He went out, closing the door behind him. He was gone perhaps five minutes, and when he returned he carried a bucket of water in one hand and a bunch of switches in the other. "The drier the heat," he said, "the more you can stand, yet the sauna is not all dry heat. We also enjoy what the Finns call the *loyly*." He put the bucket down beside the stove, and divided up the switches equally and gave me a handful. "This is the whisk," he continued, "which is the next step. They are birch, and should always be slightly damp. Whisking gets blood moving to the surface of the skin and helps to heat the body properly. Start at the shoulders and whisk yourself fairly briskly down to the soles of your feet. It's particularly important if you are going in the lake."

I watched him, and then started to tap my skin smartly with the switches. When he stopped, I stopped. It was too dark in the sauna to see the color of my skin but I imagined it was red. My friend then explained that since the creation of perspiration was one of the primary purposes of the sauna, this could sometimes be increased by throwing a small amount of water on the rocks. The *loyly,* as the Finns call it, is often described as "the exquisite tingle" because sauna bathers feel a hot, tingling sensation on the skin a few seconds after the water touches the stones. Aarne suggested I change shelves with him, as the *loyly* would be more pronounced on the higher berth. I moved my towel to the top shelf, and stretched out again. I heard the water sizzle on the stones and about three seconds later the steam struck me. My first sensation was that the heat had surely doubled; I gasped. Then I felt as though a hundred needles were pricking my skin, but it was oddly pleasant. In a few seconds it was over. I sat up. "Can we do that again?" I asked. Aarne laughed, and dipped another ladle on the rocks. Sitting up, the effect of the *loyly* was even more intense. I could hardly breathe. But the tingle was one of those sweet-sour combinations that, like a color, is impossible to describe.

"Actually, the temperature rose very little if at all when I put the water on the rocks," Aarne said. "But it certainly seems hotter. *Loyly* should be used sparingly, or else humidity makes the air heavy and not so pleasant. This happens often in public saunas." I asked how long a sauna should last, and Aarne replied that it depended upon the taste of the individual. "Stay only as long as you are enjoying it," he said. "We've been in here about twenty minutes, and I'm ready for the lake now."

Aarne opened the door, raced along the dock, and dived with a clumsy splash into the lake. I knew the swim was inevitable but I dreaded the shock of the cold water, and I hesitated. At the end of the dock I paused again, then closed my eyes and dived. There was no shock at all; as I swam to the surface the water did not even seem terribly cold. Aarne was climbing up a ladder at the end of the dock, and I followed him. "Your body was very warm and that cushioned you against the normal shock you would have felt," he said. "Now back to the sauna for some more heat." We stayed in the sauna about ten minutes, and then dived again into the lake. When we climbed up the ladder, I started toward the dressing room. "Wait," Aarne said. "Don't towel off. Let your skin dry in the air." It was late in the afternoon of an autumn day and already there was a slight chill in the air but I did not feel the least discomfort as we waited there in front of the dressing room for our bodies to dry. Aarne said that even when he bathed in the snow, in the middle of winter, he never used a towel but stood in the cold air until all the water had evaporated from his skin. "I don't know what it does," he said, "but you'll feel better for having done it."

We dressed slowly. Sometimes, Aarne said, he took a few eggs into the sauna with him and when he came out the eggs were hard cooked, and he would eat them as he dressed. "I didn't today," he said, "because my wife is fixing a special stew for dinner, and I didn't want to dull your appetite." It was almost dark when we started back along the path to the house. I felt drowsy, relaxed, and utterly at peace. Neither of us spoke until we reached the house.

In the living room, Aarne brought out a bottle of aquavit

and poured us both a drink. He tossed it down in a swallow, and I did the same. It was fiery and brought tears to my eyes. "We will have dinner now," he said, "or otherwise you will fall asleep." The stew was superb; it was flavored with anise and while I have not the slightest idea what it contained I devoured it ravenously. For dessert there was a sort of crepe filled with cloudberries and sprinkled with sugar. It was served hot and, like the stew, it was delicious. I declined coffee, and gently pushed my chair back.

"Since the oil lamps are not very good for reading," Aarne said, "we usually go to bed early. So don't hesitate to do the same." I arose, shook hands with them both, and started toward my room. "The sauna was wonderful," I said weakly. Aarne walked with me to my room and lit a lamp. It cast a soft, warm glow over the room. "We'll have time for another tomorrow before your steamer leaves," he said. "Sleep well."

I remember taking off my clothes and I think I remember getting in the lower bunk. And then slumber locked me in an embrace that was as complete as anything I have ever experienced.

13

One-Day Castaway

CHERISHED dreams die lingering deaths: the fantasy of an uninhabited South Pacific island has always haunted me. In my mind's eye I could see myself walking a deserted beach at sundown searching for driftwood and coconuts or netting fish in a blue lagoon or whiling away the hot, languid hours by paddling about naked in the freshwater pool under the waterfall.

In French Polynesia, I asked a friend who worked for the government if he could arrange to have me put ashore for a day on an uninhabited island near Bora-Bora. "You will go crazy if you aren't already," he replied. "Make it a couple of hours instead." I insisted. It must be a full day. I wanted an island with shade, some coconut palms, a beach, and if possible, fresh water. I wanted to wade ashore at first light in the morning, and I wanted to be picked up at sundown. For twelve hours I wanted to be forgotten, a castaway. He shook his head in bewilderment and went away, saying he would inquire around and find out what would be the best island for the adventure.

Later that evening he came to my hotel at Bora-Bora. I was on the verandah drinking a gin and tonic. "I've found an island for you," he said, "but it doesn't have fresh water. At least no one knows whether it has fresh water or not. No one has been very far inland and I doubt if you will go either because there are wild pigs there. But if there are pigs, there must be drinking water. However, don't be foolish. Take food and water." He clapped his hands for service and pointed toward my drink and said something in Polynesian. In a moment he was raising his glass to me. "Good luck," he said. "I wouldn't spend a whole day on that island alone for a full week's salary." I asked him the name of the island. "It doesn't have a name that I know of," he said. "Who wants to name a clump of coconut palms?"

I got up at four o'clock the next morning. It was still dark as I walked along the gravel walk from my bungalow to the main hotel building. The jasmine was still open and the early morning air was filled with the scent of the blossoms. The aroma of jasmine travels in tantalizing waves; one smells it one moment, and in the next it is gone. I went into the kitchen and found a boy sweeping the floor. He pointed to my food and water basket — a pathetically small package, it struck me at the time — and set about to prepare a cup of coffee. I ate a banana, drank the coffee, and carrying the basket, I went out on the porch to await the car that was to take me to the dock. The driver was punctual. He told me in French that he would pick me up that night at the dock about eight o'clock. The dawn began to break as we drove along the coast road to Vaitape, the village where I was to take the boat. It was cool, but I knew enough about the islands to know that in a couple of hours it would be hot. We drove past the tiny, white church, and through the village's single street. At the dock we both got out of the car and he carried my basket to the boat, which was bobbing in the gentle swell. The boatman smiled and said something in Polynesian, which I assume was a greeting. I said, "Bon jour," and jumped into the boat. The driver handed me the basket and untied the line. The boatman started the motor, and in a few minutes the village and Pofai Bay were falling behind us. We had been going about forty-five minutes when the boatman said something and pointed ahead. There seemed to be a half-dozen islands on the horizon and I couldn't tell which one he was pointing to. When I pointed at one, he shook his head vigorously and began to flap his arms like wings. I gathered that was a bird sanctuary. As I pointed to the various islands he flapped at them all except one. That was my island.

He came in as close as he could without going aground, then jumped into water about waist-deep and steadied the boat for me. I took off my wristwatch and put it in a shirt pocket and buttoned the flap. Then I jumped into the water, and reached under the seat and retrieved my basket. The water was cool but not unpleasantly so. The boatman smiled and said, "*A sept heures.*" I said, "*D'accord,*" and turned and started wading toward land.

My first disappointment was that I had been put ashore not on a beach but on a coral strand. Since I had kept on my shoes, I was able to walk on the coral but it was uneven and I had to walk with caution. Land, when I reached it, was also coral, which is beautiful underwater but about as exciting and inert as lava when exposed. When I looked back at the boat, it was rapidly becoming a small object on the horizon. I was alone.

I don't know what I had imagined I would do first if I were ever put ashore on a deserted island, but I'm sure I didn't do it. What I actually did was place the basket of food and water in the shade of some pandanus plants, and then I came back to the open space by the water's edge, removed my trousers, wrung the seawater from them, and placed them on the coral rocks to dry. I couldn't tell if the tide was rising or falling, and while it probably didn't matter much, I decided it was the sort of thing a man should know. I placed a stone that I would recognize at the point where the last wave had touched, and I figured to use that to determine tidal action. Then I took out my watch and strapped it to my wrist. It was 6:40.

About two hundred feet from where I had waded ashore, the coral rose to a high promontory and I decided to start my exploration there. I climbed carefully to the top of the ledge, and looked around. Only a narrow strait, about the length of a football field, separated me from the nearest island, which I assumed was one of the bird sanctuaries. A submerged reef seemed to join the two islands together. On the other side of the rock ledge was more coral and no sign of sand. As far as I could see, which was no more than a few hundred feet since the island curved sharply, there was nothing but a forest of coconut palms, coral and the sea. I turned and went back to my arrival point. My government friend had told me there was a sand beach on the island; I decided the best way to find it would be to go inland and come out on the other side.

If the romance of the adventure had not already started to fall apart, it did at that moment. A flock of frigate birds came out of the trees and began dive-bombing me with the most raucous screams I have ever heard from a bird, and when I retreated to cover I saw two enormous land crabs crawling across the top of my food basket, searching for an entry point. The crabs scampered back into their holes when I struck at them with a stick, but from the way the ground was pocked with holes I knew there were others that were awaiting their chance. Obviously, wherever I went I would have to carry the basket with me. The birds flew in a tight circle over my head, ready to resume their attack when I came out in the open again. I moved the basket as far from the crab holes as I could get, and sat on a fallen palm log. I was off to a bad start.

It was obvious that I was too close to the birds' nesting area, so I made a quick run into the open to get my trousers, then picked up the basket, and started moving cautiously through the underbrush around the edge of the coral. I felt foolish being frightened by a flock of birds, but their initial bombing run had seemed completely businesslike and I didn't care to see what they had in mind for me if I reappeared in the open. The growth was much denser than I had imagined it would be, and there were crabholes everywhere, including one monstrous one at least six inches in diameter. Moreover, the sun was moving higher in the sky and I was beginning to feel the heat. Where was the freshwater pool and the waterfall, the white beach, the blue lagoon, the trade winds?

It took a half-hour or more to get to a point where I could no longer see or hear the birds and, still carrying the basket and my trousers, I stepped out into the open and walked to the water's edge. There was still no sign of sand, but I knew I had covered only a very small part of the island's circumference. Again, I spread my trousers out on the rocks and decided to use them as my guidepost on the island. The boatman would pick me up that night where he had put me ashore, and I needed some point of orientation. Already, everything on the island had begun to look alike.

I realized I was thirsty, and I opened the basket and took out the water bottle. It was smaller than I expected. I removed the cap and took a couple of swallows. I would have to conserve water unless I could open some coconuts and so far the only coconuts I had seen were waterlogged ones floating partly submerged in the surf. It was getting steadily warmer, and I had grown tired of the sharp coral. I wanted to get to a beach where I could swim, and stretch out in the sand. I decided to head inland and get across to the other side.

Stepping into the palm forest was like stepping into a cathedral. The sun was suddenly gone, and the air was totally still. The undergrowth — mostly pandanus — was much thicker than I had thought it would be, and the ground was covered with guano and rotting vegetation. My foot sank in this about six inches with every step I took. Sometimes the pandanus grew in such dense clumps that I had to circle them. I had the feeling that everything in that suffocating jungle forest was hostile, and I grew jumpy at mysterious rustlings in the fallen fronds. I wondered if it were possible that the island was big enough for me to get lost on, but I looked back and saw that my tracks were well marked and could guide me back to the sea with no trouble. I discovered very soon that I had made a major mistake in leaving my trousers, as the pandanus fronds were sharp and in places they grew so profusely it was impossible to skirt them. The air was heavy and I began to sweat profusely.

I don't know when it was that I became aware of a noise ahead of me; it was one of those minor sounds that one hears for a while before it penetrates the conscious mind. I stopped in my tracks and listened. It was audible now: things were moving — some distance away — in the forest. Then I heard a high-pitched squeal, followed by more scampering. Of course, the wild pigs. They seemed dead ahead, so I veered slightly toward the left. I doubted that they were dangerous, but I preferred to avoid them if possible. I stopped for another drink from the bottle — it was almost half empty now — and then pushed on. My shirt was soaked with perspiration, and my feet were covered with jungle filth halfway to my knees.

And then suddenly I stepped out of the forest. In front of me was the sea, with gentle rollers coming up on a beach that seemed to slope hardly at all. I was momentarily dazzled by the brilliance of the sun and the water, and then I dropped the basket, unbuttoned my shirt and threw it in the sand, and ran into the water. I swam, I dived, I floated, and once I remember, I stood on my head. It was wonderful, and for at least an hour I gloried in the splendor of it. Then I came out and, naked, flopped in the sand. I think I slept.

The sun was almost directly overhead when the heat drove me back into the shade but not back into the forest. I found a small clump of palms very close to the water's edge, and I settled there. Opening the food basket, I was pleased to find half a roast chicken, a ripe mango, several slices of bread, and a paper napkin. I recoiled slightly at the latter; it seemed incongruous on a desert island. I dug a hole in the sand and buried it. Later I interred the chicken bones and the mango seed beside the napkin; if civilization was coming to the island it would not be in the form of littering.

It was perhaps an hour later that out of the blue came a strange realization: I was bored. I went back into the sea and repeated my water sports, but the original zest was lacking. I gazed at the next island in the chain — it was about a quarter of a mile away — and pondered whether or not I would swim to it if I saw a native girl on the beach there. I decided I would. But like my own island, it showed no sign of life. I got up and decided to walk around the other side of the island as far as I could, but once away from the beach there was the same lifeless coral that had driven me away from my first landing spot. I wished I had brought something to read. It was 2:49; almost five hours to go.

I went back to the shade of the palm trees and slumped down in the sand. Suppose the boatman forgot to come back for me, or suppose some accident befell him and no one would know that he had even brought me here. My water was down to a few swallows; my food was gone. What would I do? I would stalk a wild pig, I decided, and spear it with a sharp stick, after tracing it to its watering hole. But my friend in the government knew where I was and when I failed to show up at the hotel, he would send someone for me. There was no danger.

During the next couple of hours, I tried to climb a palm tree, and failed; I tried to drive an ugly-looking fish into a tiny pool behind a sandbar, and failed; and I tried to start a fire by reflecting the sun from my watch crystal. That didn't work either, but the three efforts brought me to five o'clock. I felt better, but thirsty; all of my water was gone.

I took one more swim, dried off in the sun, put on my shirt and shoes, and plunged again into the jungle forest. It was easy to follow my trail, but it was even hotter and more oppressive than it had been earlier that morning. When I came out of the forest, I saw my trousers spread out on the coral and they seemed like an old friend. I put them on; the sun was dropping low and I could expect my boatman to appear any time. It was nearly seven o'clock.

The mosquitoes arrived before the boatman; at first just a few and then they began to swarm. I turned up my shirt collar and sought to protect my head and hands. This wasn't altogether successful, and I was about to wade into the water when I heard the sound of a motor. It was the boat, still some distance away but it signaled the arrival of a civilization I had so happily discarded twelve hours earlier. I slapped at the mosquitoes, and waited.

14

From Key Largo to Key West

S OUTH of Miami, south of Homestead, the John D. Mac-Donald country of cinder-block houses with plastic venetian blinds and Parrot Jungles and Orchid Gardens falls behind, and at the tip of the Florida peninsula there is nothing but scrub brush, sky, and a desolate hint of the Everglades. Gone are the pink plaster flamingos, the serpentariums, the Seminole villages and the retirement colonies called Bali Hai, Catalina and Acapulco, and ahead are the twenty-nine islands and forty-two bridges across which the Overseas Highway — the romantic name for the southernmost section of Route 1 — sweeps in a 120-mile westerly arc to Key West.

They will tell you in Florida that there are, in all, 362 keys, most of them uninhabited, where the Atlantic Ocean and the Gulf of Mexico come together, but the figure has little meaning. Some are no more than clumps of red mangrove, whose roots rest in shallow water, and others are exposed reefs. It doesn't matter. The sea is dotted with islands but the only ones easily accessible are those reached by the narrow two-lane highway that was erected on what was left of Henry Flagler's railroad after the hurricane of

1935. On one side of the road are the generally calm waters of the Gulf; on the other side the inshore ocean flats are light green, a sharp contrast to the deep blue of the Gulf Stream that flows northward a few miles offshore.

I am at Key Largo and the stars are out, although it rained intermittently all the way from Miami and the rhythmic sweep of the windshield wipers made me drowsy and I once dozed off and almost drove into a swamp. The stout lady at Hilda's German Motel said, "It's snowing in New York. I just heard it on the radio." She seemed pleased. Later that evening I followed her directions and went across the road to have dinner at Captain Doug's Blue Marlin Restaurant, where the shrimp were fine but everything else seemed to have been fried in deep fat and tasted alike. After eating, I bought a bottle of beer and walked aimlessly down a sand road to the edge of the Gulf. There was a decrepit wharf there, and I walked out as far as I thought safe, took off my shoes, and let my feet dangle in the water. There was scarcely a ripple on the surface of the water, and far offshore I could see lights from the shrimp fleet. It was very quiet and very dark, and for some reason I suddenly thought of Maxwell Anderson's beautiful verse play *Key Largo*. The setting was something like this, I remembered: an old dock, some palmettos lining a crushed-shell roadway, the shrimp boats out in the Gulf. All that was lacking was the rickety one-story house with palm thatch, and the Spanish bayonet growing out front, where the blind man and his daughter lived. I thought for a moment and her name came back to me: Alegre. I walked back to the motel carrying my shoes in my hand. Some newcomers had arrived and were being shown the room next to mine. I heard Hilda tell them it was snowing in New York.

The Gulf Stream is fifty miles wide and two thousand feet deep with a rate of flow 1,000 times that of the Mississippi River. Moving around the Florida Keys and up the Atlantic Coast its speed exceeds four knots, but beyond Cape Hatteras it broadens, slackens, and begins to meander. Its high salt content, warmer temperature, and indigo color distinguish it from the inshore counter current along the east coast. The offshore boundary of the Gulf Stream is less clearly defined.

The mounted, blue-lacquered sailfish and the trailer are the trademarks of the Keys. In the dining room of the Holiday Inn at Marathon there was not one but six curving sailfish on the walls, while the trailer parks are so numerous that at times they seem to touch, blend together, and form one enormous complex stretching to the horizon. The trailer villages have names like Venetian Shores, Bahamas and — incredibly — Cape Cod South, and the word *trailer* does not appear to have been banished here as it has in so many places. Still, mobile-home villages seem the most popular designation, although R. V. Resorts and Rec-Vee Parks are coming on strong. Advertisements for condominiums, and there must be thousands of such structures in the Keys, run rampantly to hyperbole, culminating in the Summer Sea, which is described simply as "too beautiful for words." It didn't look like it to me but I'm harsh in my judgment of condominiums.

At breakfast on Plantation Key I was offered my choice of hominy grits or home-fries, one of those minor geographical signposts that remind the traveler where he is. It was becoming hot when I backed out of the parking lot and waited my turn to cut into the endless stream of highway traffic. Windley Key and Upper and Lower Matecumbe Keys are devoted to fishing as though nothing else exists. Hundreds of small marinas on both the ocean and Gulf shores advertise rods, reels, tackle, ice and dockage. And beer. Fishermen drink a lot of beer.

I pause for the night at Ruttger's on Key Colony Beach. Key Colony is a small island that isn't on the Overseas Highway, but is connected to Marathon Key by a bridge. Ruttger's is a three-story motel, clean and airy, with a fairly good beach on the Atlantic. At sundown I walked out on a fishing pier under the brooding scrutiny of three pelicans roosting on pier poles. I threw half a doughnut to one, who caught it with no trouble in midair. The other two regarded me with looks of injury, and I went back to my room and brought the box out and divided up the doughnuts as evenly as possible. None of them looked pleased at the division.

> *The pelican is the waterfowl of the Florida Keys. The lower half of its enormous beak is a pouch, which it uses for catching fish but contrary to general opinion it is not used for storage. A silent and brooding bird, it crash lands in the water when diving for fish but is protected from injury by an air cushion. Even the California and Texas pelicans winter in the Florida Keys, where they breed in large colonies. When hatched — which takes about a month — the young pelican is totally naked.*

I find that much of the travel through the Keys is a journey of persuasion: buy a condominium, buy a trailer site, buy a vacation home. Anything enclosed in four walls seems to be a "villa" and wherever possible a noun is modified by the adjective "tropical." All breezes are tropical, all plants including geraniums are tropical, and all nights, skies, and sunsets are tropical.

Whale Harbor separates Windley Key from Upper Matecumbe Key, and here the islands begin to look like keys. Often the waters of the Atlantic lap one side of the road, while the somewhat bluer Gulf can be seen through the mangroves on the other side. On a sunny day the glare is intense. It is ten-thirty in the morning, and already traffic is building up to an almost steady flow, and I note that the 45 m.p.h. speed limit that has prevailed in the upper keys has given way to 55 m.p.h. Wishing to loiter, I moved in behind a Daytona 500 Swinger and kept well below 55. The bridge beyond Craig Key gives an unobstructed view of the Gulf and I was surprised at the number of low-lying islands that stood out in relief against the horizon. There were dozens of them, low to the water, green, covered with mangrove trees, and undoubtedly submerged during hurricanes.

At Duck Key, I pulled off the Overseas Highway to take a look at Indies Inn and Yacht Club, which is said to possess the most elegant accommodations south of Miami. The report is probably true. The hotel itself somewhat resembles the Greenbrier at White Sulphur Springs, West Virginia; the golf course is well maintained, the all-weather tennis courts are handy to the main building, and for yachtsmen there are boatel suites and marina villas with kitchen facilities. Rates at the hotel in winter season (December 21 to April 26) are $44 a day for what is referred to as an Indies Apartment of one bedroom and bath, without meals. This drops to $28 a day out of season. A marina apartment, overlooking the harbor and consisting of a bedroom, bath, kitchen and living room, is also $44 a day during the winter season, dropping to $28 off season. The price seems right, but a minimum of two days' occupancy is required.

> *"That's a nice looking vehicle," says a man in the parking lot of the restaurant. "What is it?"*
> *"It's a Winnebago Brave," the owner replied.*
> *"Want to trade it for a Layton that's only been to Pennsylvania and back?"*
> *"Probably not," the owner replied, "but I'll take a look at the Layton."*

There aren't many palm trees in the Keys, but one small stretch of highway just before Marathon boasted both palms and a few flashes of bougainvillea, which came with the relief of a thunderstorm after a drought. Mangrove and scrub growth become unbearably monotonous after a while. At Grassy Key, I turned into Flipper's Sea School, where for a three-dollar admission I saw Gipper, a twenty-seven-year-old dolphin, find and retrieve a quarter thrown in thirty-five feet of water. As Sarasota is the winter training quarters for the Ringling Bros. and Barnum & Bailey Circus, Flipper's Sea School seems to be the same sort of thing for the sea worlds scattered around the country. The dolphins and sea lions put on a hell of a performance under a fierce noonday sun, but I would risk sunstroke anytime to see Gipper break water with that quarter balanced on his head and a sly grin on his face. After the show was over, the master of ceremonies said he would answer questions about dolphin behavior, and a half-dozen questions were asked immediately. I wondered, not for the first time, why all questions on these occasions are invariably idiotic.

Crawl Key is small, but not so small that it didn't possess the standard Key institutions: Ed's Bike Shop, Whispering

Pines Trailer Park, Capt. Mike Hill's Fresh Shrimp Daily, Pirate's Torture Museum, Sarah's Efficiencies — Color TV, and the Tru-Art Studios. Very compact but very complete.

Marathon, which is a bit more than halfway to Key West, is the largest town encountered, and is further distinguished by an airport whose runway parallels the road. Air Sunshine flies DC-3's from Miami International Airport several times a day, and during the winter the fifty-five-minute flights are almost invariably sold out. The Sombrero Reef Club, on Marathon, berths some enormous yachts, on one of which — the *White Sands* — I was invited by the owners for cocktails. We sat on deck enjoying the cool (tropical) evening while the sun (tropical) dipped out of sight. There were no mosquitoes and it was pleasant. A radio on an adjacent yacht was sending some Cole Porter music in our direction, and the owner made some equally pleasant sounds as he dropped ice in glasses and poured drinks. He was heading back to Maryland the next day, but he explained that he came to Marathon every winter for no reason more important than that he liked it. Later we walked from the slip to the Sombrero Country Club for dinner, where an orchestra was playing for dancing. It was a typical small country club, the men in sports jackets and blazers, the women in long dresses. Marathon is 111 miles from Miami in distance but fifty years away in time.

There are said to be six hundred varieties of fish in the waters adjacent to the Florida Keys, but those most commonly sought by fishermen are snook, tarpon, snapper, redfish, bonefish, grouper, grunts, jewfish, queen triggers, yellowtail, angelfish, sailfish,

> *marlin, dolphin (fish — not the porpoise), sharks, and*
> *tuna. No license is required for saltwater sports fish-*
> *ing. Turtles, manatees, manta rays, and porpoise are*
> *protected by Florida law.*

A little bit south of Marathon is Seven Mile Bridge, the longest overwater stretch on the Overseas Highway. Built over shallow coral reefs, the bridge — if traffic isn't too heavy — gives a fine view of the sea, the islands, and the hundreds of fishing boats working the area. The bridge actually begins at Vaca Key and passes high over Pigeon Key, a tiny island of palm trees and a few white buildings belonging to the University of Miami School of Environmental Studies. At Bahia Honda, I pulled in to the State Recreation Area which for a twenty-five-cent admission offers bathhouses, boat rentals, diving supplies, a small marina, a bait and tackle shop, and access to a dreadful beach. I stretched out on a seawall in the sun and watched a couple snorkel, but they didn't seem to find anything more interesting under water than I had found on land.

I left the highway again at Big Pine Key looking for the tiny deer said to be the size of a collie that inhabit the swamps and palmetto thickets of the island, but I couldn't even find the Key Deer Refuge although I drove around in a circle trying to follow the signs that seem to have been arranged in a way to drive visitors insane. I gave up when I passed the Baptist Church the second time. A few more islands, mostly given over to billboards advertising Key West restaurants and motels, and I crossed the small bridge connecting Stock Island and Key West.

> *Key West — a corruption of the Spanish* Cayo Hueso
> *— is an island two miles wide by four miles long, and*
> *has a population of 55,000 people. For a long time the*

island was linked to Havana, only ninety miles away, by car ferries and this, together with the cigar factories that once were the principal business of the island, attracted a large Cuban population. Bahamanians came, and fishermen, spongers, wreckers, and adventurers. And, finally, Ernest Hemingway and Tennessee Williams.

The Pier House Hotel, at the foot of Duval Street, has been strikingly restored and dominates Old Town Square. It is a remarkable hotel, rambling vaguely about the waterfront and intruding even upon the dock, and although a large part of it is quite new it somehow manages to *seem* old. On my first night in Key West, I ordered a vodka and tonic spiced with a Key lime and carried it from the bar, through the verandah café, and outside to the sea. Skirting the building, I found a large rock at the water's edge and from the top of the rock I watched the sun go down. Sunsets in Key West are extraordinarily spectacular, I don't know why. The clouds turn from pink to gray, like a piece of coral lifted from the sea. The sun drops quickly and the water, a moment ago blue, is suddenly dark green. The offshore islands become shapeless blurs on the horizon. A man on a sailfish, standing, scudded rapidly across the harbor, and a dog on a moored sloop stood up suddenly and barked as the sailfish sped past. A light breeze arose, rattling the halyards of the sailboats. It was a fine moment.

The food in Key West is generally good, especially the shrimp and fish, and it was unfailingly good at the Pier House. On my second day there I walked a couple of blocks along Duval Street to a Cuban restaurant called El Cacique, which makes a specialty of yellow rice and chicken, and paella. The black bean soup and shrimp enchilada were excellent, so much so that I topped it with a Cuban sandwich and a wedge of Key lime pie. Chez Emile, on the balcony of Harbor House, serves first-rate French food, and Fogarty, on Duval Street, is fair, although the mansion in which the restaurant is located is magnificent. The restaurant that disappointed me the most was the Buttery, which possesses a good reputation and which I am prepared to excuse on the grounds that I arrived for dinner quite late and most of the specialties were gone from the menu.

In the fierce heat of noon one day I wandered into the Peggy Mills Garden, in Old Town, and it was like stepping into a jungle. After ten steps I felt swallowed up and wondered if I could find my way back to the street again. There is something wonderfully deceptive about the size of that garden; it isn't really all that grand but it somehow — with its winding paths and tiny pools — gives the impression of being endless. I found a bench in a glade and sat for a while. Two people, speaking Spanish, walked by with cameras, but I was otherwise alone. It was cool under the dense foliage and remarkably quiet considering the street was only a stone's throw away. When I left, a lady at the gate thrust a pamphlet in my hand which said the garden had been started in 1930, that the bricks in the path were all over a hundred years old, and that most of the plants were rare in that they would grow outdoors nowhere else in the United States. I'm sure that's all true, but the charm of the place, to me, was that once in the garden the rest of the world seemed tightly sealed off. Sometimes that's a real prize.

For an admission fee of one dollar, the Book-of-the-Month Club and Literary Guild subscriber can visit the Ernest Hemingway house on Whitehead Street where the author wrote *For Whom the Bell Tolls, A Farewell to Arms,* "The Snows of Kilimanjaro," and *Green Hills of Africa,* among others. Hemingway owned the house from 1931 until his death in 1961, but he lived at a great many other places during this period. Local gossip has it that he spent a good part of his nonworking hours on a barstool at Sloppy Joe's, which is now Captain Tony's, on Greene Street, but these stories undoubtedly enlarge with the passage of time. Nonetheless, Hemingway was certainly no stranger to bars around the world, and he very likely may have refreshed himself regularly at Captain Tony's. The Hemingway house, a two-story Spanish colonial structure of native rock with a second-story verandah, is one of the most attractive homes on the island. The dwelling of Tennessee Williams, at 1431 Duncan Street, is quite modest compared to the Hemingway house. An attractive, compact little house painted white with red shutters, it has a small gazebo in the front and a swimming pool in the backyard. Comfortable-looking but unpretentious. At 608 Angela Street is the restored home of Philip Burton, whose protégé and namesake, Richard, has achieved some success as an actor in London and New York. Burton, a world-famous theatrical coach, is something of a recluse in Key West, although he emerges from time to time to give a lecture on the theater.

The Audubon House, on Whitehead Street a few blocks from Hemingway's house, is a magnificent building that now contains some of John J. Audubon's original drawings, all of which are said to have been made from dead birds. How the great ornithologist came into the possession of so many dead birds is a subject, like family ghosts and scandals, that the keepers of the Audubon House don't particularly care to discuss.

[131]

The Overseas Fruit Market advertises that it sells all kinds of exotic fruits, but the last week in February it had nothing more exotic than bananas. When I asked for Key limes, the lady shook her head. "It's Key lime season," she acknowledged, "but they are all bought up." I said I'd take a few Persian limes. "Why not?" she said agreeably. "Everybody else does." So much for Key limes.

I drive slowly down South Street toward the very end of the United States. There is great competition to be the southernmost anything. There is the southernmost motel, the southernmost pharmacy and, for all I know, the southernmost proctologist. South Street is pleasant, and at its end is an outdoor shell market that is not only the southernmost in the country but also probably the biggest. It is besieged by tourists examining conch shells in close detail, which puzzles me because I feel when you see one conch shell you've pretty much seen them all. I know very little about shells and have no particular desire to add to my knowledge.

Slightly to the west of the southernmost tip is the United States Naval Base, which President Truman found so much to his liking that he located his winter White House there. The Truman presence has never been taken lightly in Key West. Truman Avenue is one of the city's main boulevards, and one day while driving aimlessly about the city I came upon — to my delight — the Margaret Truman Launderette. Fame touches, sometimes lightly, those upon whom it bestows its favor.

The southernmost beach is on the Atlantic Ocean at the foot of Simontown Street. There is a cluster of large motels here, and one enters the beach through the entrance to the Sands Restaurant, where a fifty-cent admission is charged.

The water was cloudy and the beach was littered with seaweed. The best swimming in Key West is found in swimming pools.

> *"The trouble with Key West," said the lady on the Conch train to nobody in particular, "is that this is where the hippies went." The Conch train takes tourists on a sightseeing trip of the entire island. It was a Sunday, and the lady seemed to have a point although on other days there did not seem to be many hippies around. But on Sundays, Old Town looked like the Haight-Ashbury in the sixties. Clad in the uniform of blue jeans, headbands, and sandals, they presided over sidewalk stalls of belts, cheap jewelry, shells, candles, and wood carvings. Some just stood around. A beardless person in Old Town on a Sunday is a freak.*

The black man at the turtle kraal is a real showman. The kraal is located near the docks where the shrimp boats tie up, and it consists of a few large saltwater pens, one or two covered ones, a museum of sorts, and the inevitable gift shop. It costs one dollar to enter and although the turtles put on a predictably lethargic performance, the man makes sure you get your money's worth. His lecture — delivered with sly grins and a conspiratorial manner — ranges the entire breadth of marine biology and is delivered with such gusto and unconcealed delight that it's hard not to be swept along.

The invitation to the cocktail party said seven o'clock. It was dark when I arrived at the house on Grinnel Street but not so dark I couldn't recognize it as very imposing. The guests were milling through the first floor rooms, in the manner that cocktail guests circulate everywhere, and spilling out on the rear lawn. There was an immense indoor swimming pool in a separate building; someone said the roof folded back in good weather, but I was skeptical.

"We aren't too involved in Florida affairs," an attractive woman in a white jumpsuit said, "unless they affect Key West. I get the *Miami Herald*, but some days I just can't get up enough interest to read it. I don't know whether that's good or bad."

"Reading the *Miami Herald?*" I asked.

"No," she said. "Being self-contained the way we are. But that's what comes from living on an island."

Most of the guests, I noticed, were middle-aged and expensively dressed, and they drank as though they enjoyed it. The party lasted late.

On my last morning in Key West, I arose early and walked down to the Fisherman's Café on Caroline Street for breakfast. The Cuban coffee was explosive. The morning was not yet hot, so after eating I wandered over to the shrimp boats. One of the boats, the *Martha J.*, was getting ready to go out, and its deck was a scene of furious activity. A swarthy man in a cook's cap came out of a door and leaned against the railing. He waved at me and I waved back. Night trawling, I was told, brings far greater hauls than daytime shrimp fishing, and a lot of the trawlers lie tied up all day.

At Sloppy Joe's I asked for a bloody mary. It is morning but the bar is nearly full. Most are tourists. They sit under the big overhead fans looking expectantly, but nothing happens. The jukebox is playing something with a Latin beat and the volume is turned up high. The bartender is young and polite. "I hope you like that, sir," he said as he placed the bloody mary on the bar. I didn't. A good bloody mary is hard to make.

After lunch I edged again into the Overseas Highway traffic and headed north. I drove as fast as traffic permitted, and well before dark I reached Key Largo. There was a vacancy sign at Hilda's German Motel, and I pulled in. Hilda offered to show me my room, but I said it wasn't necessary. "I hear it's snowing in New York," she said.

15

A Simple Pique-nique

An old European proverb says that half the journey is getting out of the inn. I accept that as the beginning of all travel wisdom, but equally important, I contend, is not loitering around too long for lunch. One of the quickest ways to lunch well, and also to lunch economically, is the roadside picnic. It is a *pause* in the journey, not a complete stop.

Of course, there are picnics that are movable feasts, with assorted hors d'oeuvres, celery remoulade, Westphalian ham, cold salmon with *sauce verte*, pâté de fois gras, Bismarck herring, cold duck, Camembert, Brie, Pont-l'Evêque, Roquefort and everything except doormen, potted palms and an orchestra, but that is not what I have in mind. A good roadside picnic, in my opinion, should be simple and inexpensive to prepare and *tout agréable* to consume. Let me explain.

Just outside Le Puy, a small French city about midway between Clermont-Ferrand and Lyons, there is an odd little mountain with a tiny village on its crown, and at the foot of that mountain is a meadow through which a stream wanders. One sunny day, in early June, I picnicked beside that stream, and although it's been a number of years ago I remember precisely what I ate, the vivid color of the scarlet poppies that grew rampantly in the meadow, the feel of the sun on my face, and the mellow, fruity taste of an undistinguished but not forgotten Côte-du-Rhône with which I washed down the sausage of Arles and the Brie and the bread and, finally, two ripe figs. The whole lunch cost an insignificant amount, and it required an expenditure in time of exactly what I wanted it to be, no more and no less. As well as I remember, I let the Brie bask in the sunlight for a short period while I lay on my back and watched the clouds. It was all over in an hour, maybe less, and I was on my way again; yet that hour has remained green in my memory ever since, although far more elaborate meals in expensive restaurants have faded entirely away. The only drawback to a picnic that occurs to me at this moment is the lamentable absence of cooking smells, those wonderful odors that speak of bouillabaisse simmering or bread baking or some mysterious stew that somewhere is bubbling in its own juice, but the blended odor of thousands of tiny blooming plants in the meadow can momentarily, at least, compensate for what you are missing.

Buy the food in the last village you pass through before you start looking for a picnic spot, although I'm not sure why I say this because refrigeration isn't important for what you are likely to get. But your appetite at this point will be keener, and this added edge to hunger will bring greater pleasure to the shopping. Sausage and cheese are excellent in both France and Italy, and they can be found in the tiniest of villages. Pâté and tinned spreads can be found anywhere, as well as olives, tomatoes, and fresh fruit. Local wines can be drawn from casks into liter bottles. A loaf of fresh bread, thoughtfully sliced into a half dozen chunks by the baker if you don't possess a knife, is all that is needed to finish things off. There should be no desperate ritual to the picnic; it is a simple meal, eaten in totally relaxed circumstances in a pleasant place.

A word about location. Preferences vary, but I feel somewhat sad for those families I see eating beside the road, because the noise and flatulence of truck traffic serves to diminish — for me anyway — the joy of eating outside. No, I think the road should be out of sight and out of mind, if this is possible, or at the very least it should be far enough away so the pounding of wheels is no longer heard or felt. A stream is nice, if only for keeping the wine chilled, and the ground should be dry and cleared. Once, just outside Brignoles, a small village near Marseilles, I picnicked with my son in a field that had been freshly mowed, and the scent of new-cut hay added a special delight to the adventure.

There are many variations to the picnic, and I have reduced it here to the simplest and cheapest formula imaginable. In Germany and the North Countries, good brown beer is often preferable to wine, but I would not suggest this in France or Italy, where the beers are poor and are overshadowed by even the new wines. Bottled mineral water is available in all the countries of Europe and at least one bottle is standard picnic stock, if only for cutting the wine for children.

Bon appétit!

16

As I Walked Down the
Streets of Mesilla

It's fashionable right now to identify a quaint town as being "straight out" of a movie. A Scottish village is straight out of *Whisky Galore*, a Vermont town is straight out of *The Trouble with Harry*, a western settlement is straight out of *High Noon*. Mesilla, which slumbers in the New Mexico desert a few miles north of El Paso and the Mexican border, is straight out of every Mexican movie ever filmed and one is tempted to peer around the sides of the buildings to make sure they are not just fronts supported in the back by buttresses. The town is called Old Mesilla by the people of the Southwest, although there is no New Mesilla that I know of. There is a Mesilla Park nearby, on the outskirts of Las Cruces, but there is no likelihood of confusing the two names, because Mesilla Park is a development of neat suburban homes, while Old Mesilla is, well, anything but that.

I drove up to the village square in Mesilla one terribly hot day toward the end of summer, and parked my car in the shade of a pecan tree. The town is made up mostly of adobe buildings which sit low to the ground, but around the square — or plaza, as it is officially called when civic pride is running high — there are some clapboard buildings, a few towering as high as two stories. On opposite sides of the square are the Galería de las Artes, which specializes in paintings and art objects of the Southwest, and a first-class bookstore. A few yards down the street from the art gallery is a building that was formerly the courthouse, and it was here that Billy the Kid was tried and sentenced to be hanged. Slightly behind it, in a building that is now a bar, was located the jail. According to a sign on the building, Billy the Kid was jailed there on five occasions. Billy's real name was William Bonney, and the cocktail lounge that occupies the area where the cells stood is called the William Bonney Room, a display of dignity one can't help applauding.

The plaza itself is small, and undoubtedly looks a great deal as it did during the time that Billy the Kid gave the town so much of his attention. But now in the center is an octagonal bandstand encircled by a yellow and red railing, and it is reached by five steps also painted yellow and red. This color combination may cause some overly sensitive visitors to feel queasy, but it doesn't seem to trouble the townspeople. Presumably, anyone who could get used to Billy the Kid can get used to a bilious color combination. The plaza also contains a water fountain, a commemorative flagpole, and a noncommemorative trash can. The place is dusty, with only a few tufts of brown grass doggedly holding their own in the scorched earth, and it all somehow speaks eloquently of the tempo and torpor of the town.

An elderly man in a plaid shirt, tan trousers, and zippered boots was sitting in the shade on the steps of the bandstand, watching two electricians stringing wires into the square. I walked over and asked him what the preparations were for.

He looked at me curiously before replying. "There's going to be a three-day fiesta," he replied, apparently satisfied with my appearance. "Speeches, and drinking, and mariachi music and a lot of dancing. It's held every year, and people come from Texas and New Mexico, and even from Mexico. A lot of Mexicans. It's a real blowout."

I asked him if he had lived in Mesilla long, and he regarded me again before replying. "If you want to talk about this town," he said, "it would be a lot more to my liking if we stepped into El Patio Bar instead of standing here in all this heat." El Patio Bar is a low building at one end of the square, and when we got there I saw that its front wall was decorated with a gloriously vivid life-sized oil painting of Billy the Kid gunning down an earlier proprietor of the bar. "This used to be called Gower's Saloon," my informant said, marching to the door, where he turned around and faced me. "Gower had offended Billy and tried to goad him into a gunfight. Gower came out of this door, like I'm standing now — look at me — and Billy was out there in the street, a little beyond where you are now, I figure. Billy told him to go back into the saloon, but Gower kept coming, like this." My new friend advanced slowly toward me, crouched in the familiar gun-drawing stance, his fingers spread apart like a woman impatient for her fingernail polish to dry. "He tried to draw first, but he was no match for Billy. Ka-choo! Ka-choo! Billy let him have it." He clutched himself in the middle, spun heavily and collapsed in the street. Lying there, he twitched in one last spasm of agony, and lay still. I glanced around to see if there were other witnesses to the drama, but the only people in sight were the two electricians, who were intent on their work, and a small boy riding a burro at the other end of the square. I noticed that my friend was lying in the same position as the Gower of the painting, which led me to the conclusion that the performance had been staged before. He got up brushing the dust from his trousers. "Billy was not convicted for that killing," he said. "He was cleared on the grounds that he shot Gower in self-defense." He led the way into the bar.

The establishment had been brought up to date since Mr. Gower's untimely passing; an air conditioner was at work somewhere in the rear. The room was rather large, and cool, dark and deserted. My friend asked for a bottle of beer, and drank it without moving the bottle from his lips. He placed it with great care on the bar, as though it might shatter. I asked him if he made a business of guiding visitors around town, and for a moment I thought he hadn't heard me. Then I saw that he was building up to a belch, and that the effort was consuming all his thought and energy. He gave it full voice, shattering the stillness of the room.

"Gives you room for another, doesn't it?" asked the bartender.

"Yes," my friend said, "but I'll have a glass of whiskey on the side. I need a little body with all of that air."

I have held to the belief for years that one volunteer is worth ten pressed men, so I primed the pump and waited. Wiping his lips with the back of his hand and pointing out his empty beer bottle to the bartender, my friend told me he had lived in Old Mesilla all of his sixty-eight years, that it was without doubt the finest town in the Southwest and quite possibly in the entire world, and that if I could see my way clear to coming back for the fiesta I would never have a moment's regret for the time and money invested. "In the old days we used to have parties in the plaza every Sunday after church," he said. "A mariachi band would get up there on the bandstand and play all afternoon and most of the night. You never heard such music. At night there would be dancing in the plaza, and we would drink home-made wine, which we bought in gallon jugs. Anybody drank too much, we'd put them under the bandstand and let them sleep it off. They'd still be crawling out of there as late as Tuesday." He was silent a moment. "Those days are gone now," he continued, "but we still have the fiesta. The tourists have started coming in here, and that's changed everything. Now everybody wants a souvenir shop."

He emptied another bottle of beer, an exercise that consumed only a moment. "This has always been a famous town," he went on. "Billy the Kid hung around here more than anyplace else. Course, he didn't live *anywhere* very long because he was only twenty-two when he was killed in 1881. But hundreds of years before Billy the Kid was born this was a famous Indian settlement, and for quite a time Mesilla was the capital of the Arizona and New Mexico Territory. But of course you knew that." He looked at me to make sure, and I told him that was a bit of information that I had not before encountered and I was glad to finally have that gap in my knowledge of American history bridged. Pleased at my admission, he continued: "The Gadsden Purchase, which set the boundary between the United States and Mexico, was worked out right here in Mesilla and was announced for the first time out there in the plaza. The Gadsden Museum is here, and if you haven't seen it, you ought to."

I took his advice and later in the day I drove to the Gadsden Museum, which was located in an undistinguished house on the outskirts of the village. More than anything else, it resembled the contents of an attic. The collection ranged from a Goldwater button to a letter written by Billy the Kid to his lawyer. I was told that the Wells Fargo Museum, on the other side of town, was more worthwhile, but it was soundly locked when I got there, and I had the impression it had been locked for some time. Old Mesilla is like that; it is mañana country.

Leaving the square, I walked the few blocks of a residential street that soon thinned out and became desert. There were only a few trees and the sun was blinding. All the houses were made of adobe, the bricks of which had weathered and run together, like chocolate ice cream melting. Under a tree beside the street a Mexican or Indian boy, stripped to the waist, was repairing a bicycle. He was handsome, with black hair and dark eyes, and he moved with the grace of an animal. He stopped work and eyed me curiously; I got the feeling that most visitors didn't get that far from the plaza.

Many people, I was told, come to Mesilla to dine at La Posta, an ancient Mexican restaurant that served for more than a hundred and fifty years as a stagecoach station on the Butterfield Train. A rambling adobe building, it has nine dining rooms where Mexican food is served by candlelight. What is now the main banquet room was once the Bean Saloon, one of the most notorious dives in the Southwest. The Lava Room was once the stable for the many stage lines moving from San Antonio and Mexico to what is now Los Angeles, and the lava from which its walls were made came from the Black Mesa, west of Mesilla. I dined in the patio, a pleasant place where cool ferns stood on tiles and waitresses in Mexican costumes bustled about. My dinner began with chile con queso and tortillas, then moved on to guacamole, rolled enchilada, tamale, rolled taco, frijoles, chili con carne, sopapillas, and for dessert an apricot empanada. It was not the best Mexican food I have ever eaten, but it was adequate, and I was soothed by the check which came to less than five dollars.

A few days later I was making an unhurried trip from Alamogordo to El Paso, and I stopped off at Old Mesilla again. I pulled up to the plaza, which was deserted except for my friend, who was dozing on the bandstand. He woke up when he heard my footsteps, and by unspoken assent we moved on to El Patio Bar. "The weather is still too hot for visitors," he said, after he had drained a bottle of beer. "Even the local people don't move around much when it's this hot. Those adobe houses are very cool because most of them have two feet of earth on the roof. Maybe the fiesta will stir things up, and pretty soon the weather will cool off and the tourists will start coming." He paused to take stock. "If you have the time, would you care to walk over to the William Bonney Room and buy me a drink while I reenact for you Billy's attempted escape from jail?" He didn't seem to have his heart in it, and I declined. "Maybe later," I said, putting some coins on the counter.

When I stepped outside, the glare struck me like a blow. I walked through the deserted plaza and got in my car. No one was in sight. More than ever Mesilla looked like something straight out of a Western movie.

17

The Two Faces of Haiti

Dusk settles quickly in Haiti because of the mountains. Suddenly it's dark, and voices come clearly across the valleys, lights flicker in the hills and villages, dogs bark. The smoke from hundreds of charcoal fires becomes one more ingredient of the evening air, and occasionally in the hills the sounds of drums are heard. Drums are more noticeable in the pit of the stomach than in the ears, and it's often hard to determine from what direction the sound is arriving. Darkness is darker in Haiti than anywhere else in the world, and I don't know why, nor do I care, because so many things about that tiny country are mysterious and, although I've traveled around it a lot, I have found few answers, and eventually I have just grown to accept it for what it is. I do know that it is fundamentally a night country, that an air of great mystery clings stubbornly to it, that great beauty and squalor exist there side by side, that it has never known good government, that it is more African than Caribbean, and that poetry, music, art, flowers, and poverty run there wildly to excess. With the possible exception of Malaysia, it is the most sensuous and exotic spot on earth. And somehow it remains Haiti — a country for Haitians — instead of an artificial backdrop in front of which the pageant of tourism unfolds.

Let me say early that Haiti is not for everyone. George Santayana once declared that "nothing is objectively impressive; things are impressive when they succeed in touching the sensibility of the observer, by finding the avenues to his brain and his heart," and I think this is a beautiful way of saying that the visitor to Haiti must come with a willingness to be touched, a desire to feel. There are no racetracks, no glamorous beaches, no freeport bargain supermarkets and almost no chic gourmet restaurants. The prizes offered by Haiti are of a different kind, a *simpler* kind, and they derive from the sun, the people, the dancing, the shockingly bright colors, the voodoo, the mystery and the spirit of a people whose ancestors freed themselves from slavery with no outside help.

I have been studying Haiti for several days now, but this is not my first trip here. I first came here twenty years ago, and many times after that, but during the days of Papa Doc Duvalier my interest waned. Now I am back, sitting on a second-floor balcony of the ridiculously rococo Hotel Oloffson, watching a summer thunderstorm. Like everything else in this odd country, the storm is bigger than life, a giant among storms, bending the palm trees in the garden, beating the crotons to the ground and stripping the bougainvillea of its blossoms. A solid wall of water is in front of me, but if my predictions are correct, it will all be over in thirty minutes, the sun will come out, the streets will be dry except for the potholes, and the bougainvillea will be the same magnificent splash of magenta it was before the storm struck. Haiti recovers quickly, whether from natural or political misfortune.

It is possible to visit Haiti at this moment in total comfort but not in style — although style, too, is coming. In Pétion-ville, the hillside suburb behind Port-au-Prince, two smart and excellent restaurants have opened under the names of Chez Gérard and La Picardie, while Habitation Leclerc, a small resort complex, has been built by Olivier Coquelin on the site of Pauline Bonaparte Leclerc's palace. It is one of the loveliest, and beyond doubt one of the most chic, hotels in the Caribbean.

The Ibo Lélé, El Rancho and Villa Créole are all located in Pétionville, and all are clean, comfortable hotels. In downtown Port-au-Prince there is this indescribable Oloff-son, a gingerbread marvel, and Castel Haiti, a block or so behind the Oloffson, which seems to add another floor every year or so. Robert Baussan, a sophisticated and per-sonable Haitian architect, has created a small resort called Ibo Beach on Cacique Island, an hour's drive along the St. Marc road from Port-au-Prince, where the seaside cabañas have a certain charm and the tennis court is the best on the island. I have found it a relaxed and informal place, and I recommend it for those who would like to get away from the heat and crowds of Port-au-Prince for a few days.

Haiti *is* hot, and often humid as well, but the heat is endurable, even in summer, and no effort is made to freeze visitors with overachieving air conditioners as in Puerto Rico. I get the impression that many people live in the streets of Port-au-Prince because the roadsides swarm with humanity, and cars speed by within inches of pedestrians. Once, while I was riding in a taxicab on the Bizoton Road, a boy was struck by the right fender of my cab and knocked down. Although the boy was writhing in pain, the driver seemed intent on delivering an angry tongue-lashing until I insisted that he help me load the boy into the car and rush him to a *clinique*. After an examination showed there were no serious injuries, I took the boy to a pharmacy, bought him the medicine recommended by the doctor and took him home. The cabdriver clearly thought I was crazy.

Haiti is a mélange, of French and Arawak, of the nineteenth century and the twentieth, of fantasy and reality, of sense and nonsense. The small wooden houses, elaborately decorated with small wooden cutouts, are certainly from some other time and place. Every yard, no matter how small, is banked with banana and mango trees, hibiscus bushes and the ubiquitous croton. Ancient buses, painted in every color imaginable and flaunting such names as La Sincérité, Carmen and Le Miracle, move through the streets, the crowd giving way grudgingly to let them pass.

Haitian houses and commercial buildings possess the most immense doors I have ever seen, and all are barred with massive iron hooks that are found nowhere else that I know of. Wildly colorful and totally undisciplined paintings decorate many walls, and music comes from nowhere. Last night in the lobby and bar of the Oloffson there was a little brown boy, beautifully naked, wandering among the tables and as far as I could tell he went unnoticed by everyone but me. Who cares about a thing so trivial?

A few days ago I took a noontime walk along the rue Chile, heading aimlessly up the hill away from the city. It was fiercely hot, and I stepped from the street to rest a moment under the shade of a giant rubber tree that shielded what had once been a very handsome house. The tiles on the porch were chipped, the concrete was crumbling, balusters were missing in the railing, the garden had returned to the jungle, but the house was still lovely in its state of decay and vanished elegance; it remained a vital fragment of the panoramic collage that all Haiti somehow manages to be. Below me, shimmering in the heat, were the rooftops of Port-au-Prince, the dusty streets, the newly painted President's Palace and, beyond a strip of blue sea, rose the purple mountains that make up the island of Gonâve. No wonder so many Haitians paint; it would be strange if they didn't.

Haitian art can be wonderful, just fair, or simply terrible, but even the worst is bold, primitive and violent. One of Haiti's best artists is Préfète Duffaut; more recently Casimir Laurent has leaped into popularity among art buyers, aided mightily by the fact that the *New York Times* used one of his paintings on the cover of its Sunday magazine. Since Haitian painters see mimicry of style as one of the lesser evils, a great many artists are now painting canvases that look very much like the work of Duffaut and Casimir.

In my opinion, the finest Haitian art can be found in the murals of Ste. Trinité, the Episcopal cathedral in downtown Port-au-Prince, where a variety of Haitian artists have demonstrated a woeful misunderstanding of Protestantism and the Old Testament but have created an endearing benediction, nevertheless. Christ, being baptized, stands on an Esso oil drum, His sanctity undisturbed.

I had hoped to avoid politics, but I suppose that was unbelievably innocent of me since the regime of the elder Duvalier created such an unfortunate image of the country throughout the world. If Duvalier ever truly had a vision of social reform, it was lost in the debris of suspicion, intrigue, summary executions and terror that characterized his early years as the country's dictator. Now the son, Jean-Claude Duvalier, occupies the Palace as *Président à vie*, and visitors arriving at the François Duvalier Airport in Port-au-Prince can read his words as they sort out their·luggage: "My father created the social revolution; I, I will create the economic revolution." Perhaps. Certainly the country is in far better condition today than it was a few years ago, and no longer do visitors look around uneasily for the Tontons Macoutes, the Secret Police, that Jean-Claude's father felt the need of.

If it appears that my affection for Haiti gets in the way of objective reporting, let me point to one thing that is a malignant distraction to any tourist there, and that is the abundance of entrepreneurs. You cannot appear on the street but that you find the inevitable entrepreneur at your elbow imploring you to use only his cab, which unaccountably is four blocks away waiting for your business; or someone earnestly importuning you to eat only at a certain restaurant to which he will take you immediately as soon as his cousin's car arrives; or someone who wants to steer you to a certain gift shop, or to procure for you a Haitian lady's favor, or to sell you a fine painting at a loss to him, or to perform some other service for which you have not the slightest need. In all fairness, too, I must point out the inadequacy of Cohata Airline, certainly one of the most listless air carriers in the world. Haitien Cohata is the life-line to Cap Haitien, the old colonial capital in the north, and never was a lifeline more tenuous. Scheduled to make the one-hour flight every Monday, Wednesday and Friday, it actually flies once a week, once every two weeks, or not at all, depending upon God-only-knows-what forces control its operation. The alternative to Cohata is a somewhat rigorous motor trip of seven hours, and this is a shame because Cap Haitien is vastly interesting. Now Air Haiti is taking over and service is better. As Cap Français in the early days of the nineteenth century it was a center of shipping, roistering and buccaneering, and it was on a mountaintop overlooking the city that Henri Christophe built his famous Citadelle La Ferrière to keep Napoleon at a distance. The citadel stands there today, darkly brooding, while at the foot of the mountain, near the village of Milot, lie the ruins of Christophe's palace, Sans Souci. Cap Haitien is a small city, totally unlike Port-au-Prince in every way, and it gives one the odd feeling that it has become frozen in time. Cannon bearing the crest of Napoleon still lie rusting in the streets, and the tempo of life there is so leisurely as to be almost undetectable. A pleasant hotel called Hôtel du Roi Christophe, completely modernized a few years ago, provides comfortable accommodations for serious students of Haitian history who take the three-hour donkey ride up the mountain trail to the citadel.

This is Haiti, where good government seems persistently to escape the country, however earnest may be the intentions of its rulers, a country so close to the heart of Africa that one of its leading lotteries is called Bolette Dahomey. Voodoo exists everywhere, even in Port-au-Prince, but it is doubtful that any white person has ever witnessed a true ceremony; those permitting visitors are invariably pure theater. Beautiful and mysterious but sometimes — blissfully — anachronistic, to those who love it, as I quite obviously do, Haiti is also irresistible.

The Other Face

WHEN Habitation Leclerc opened for its first guests in January of 1974, it set up shock waves among the older and more sedate resorts of the West Indies. I am told that almost immediately it was found wanting by Fielding's *Guide to the Caribbean*, a volume I have never so much as glanced at (it would be like Brillat-Savarin consulting *The Joy of Cooking*), but which many travelers put a lot of stock in. Nevertheless, the first visitors came back speaking of the place with what was almost awe; it was certainly something new and also something vastly different. Haiti had long had a small handful of more than adequate hotels in Pétionville but this new resort was built in the middle of the city and in not a very nice part of it at that. Moreover, the whole atmosphere of the place seemed to resemble the French Riviera far more than the Caribbean. Some travel writers who flew down for an early look at it came back with a new word: Leclerc was not only exotic but also *erotic*. It looked, some implied, as though the planners were seeking to return to that period in the past when sex was a private sport rather than a protest movement. But everyone agreed on one thing: there was nothing quite like it in the Caribbean.

I have just returned from a visit to Habitation Leclerc, and I discovered that there is indeed an unmistakable sensuality to the place. One senses it immediately, but it is the kind of sensuality that appeals to the whole person — to an appreciation of total luxury, of fine food, of flawless decoration, of excellent service, of the dreamy effortlessness of doing nothing at all but doing it well. This is no faint compliment.

The resort — and it is a cluster of villas rather than a single hotel building — has been built in the lush jungle growth that occurs when a once-elegant garden is permitted to grow wild in the tropics. Many of the ancient trees and springs existed at the time Pauline was mistress of the estate. The resort is a short distance from the Carrefours Road, the main thoroughfare that runs along the waterfront and ultimately becomes the exit eastward from the city. It has been said that Habitation Leclerc was built in the middle of the city's extensive red-light district, and while this may be an exaggeration, it is almost certainly true that there are a few cottage industries in the neighborhood. But the Leclerc estate itself is separated from the raffish area surrounding it by a high wall and, once within the compound, a different world exists.

All of the buildings making up Habitation Leclerc are constructed of stone, and the first one encountered at the end of the lane is, appropriately, *la réception*. Whether the large marble statue of the semirecumbent, seminude lady beside the reception desk is intended as a sort of subliminal symbol of management attitudes is a matter of conjecture, but guests quite soon discover that a he-governs-best-who-governs-least philosophy prevails. Behind the building that houses the reception desk is the dining room, which is lighted after dark by three of the most awesome chandeliers I have ever seen. It is a stately and richly appointed room despite its being open on two sides, a fact that scarcely penetrates the consciousness of diners because walls of tropical plants combine the effect of total containment with the even more desirable prize of natural air conditioning. One of the stone walls is covered with tapestries, and a small, cheerful bar adjoins the other wall.

The villas — and there are forty-four of them in addition to eight so-called deluxe suites — are on roads and paths that fan out in all directions behind the dining room. Each of the villas has a living room, bedroom, bath, access to a patio, and a semiprivate pool. The villas are in small clusters that provide not quite so much privacy as the management would like to think, but a great deal more than can be found at most other resorts. There are two tennis courts within the compound and one unusually large swimming pool in front, and to the side, of the dining room. This pool, a spectacular thing that can only be described on an ascending scale of extravagance, is partly circled by statues and contains a toboggan slide, a waterfall, and a partially submerged bar. Recently, sunbathing girls have taken to discarding their tops, a practice that appears to disturb no one. A luncheon is served around the pool daily, and in the evening a small Haitian band plays for the bar crowd. To make the resort complete, there is a discothèque called Hippopotamus. I went once but stayed only briefly; as in all discothèques the music struck me as strictly aleatoric. In any event, you can go just so far with a discothèque.

So much for the physical layout; let's now discuss food, which at best in the Caribbean is usually only fair. Max Putier, a former chef of the Caravelle Restaurant in New York, was brought to Leclerc as the general manager, with the result that the cuisine is said to have been raised quickly to gourmet level. This, in itself, is an uncertain state, varying from individual to individual, but I can attest to the fact that several weeks after Monsieur Putier's arrival, the food in the dining room was excellent. Maybe that's gourmet level; I'm not sure. Putier has now moved on, but a recent visitor found the standards still extremely high.

Breakfast is served to guests in the patios beside the pools and is prepared in kitchens hidden away somewhere in the villa complexes. On the morning of my first day at Habitation Leclerc I stepped outside the villa and a waiter apparently had been waiting all night for me there with a glass of orange juice. He escorted me to a table shielded from the sun by a huge mango tree, and within five minutes a first-rate breakfast of eggs, bacon, fresh fruit, hot croissants and coffee was set before me. This is a fine way to start the day and I can't recommend it too highly.

Aside from the tennis courts, swimming pools and a game room containing a billiard table, there is not much within the Leclerc estate in the way of sports. Fishing, sailing, skin diving, water-skiing and snorkeling can be arranged, but the nearest beach is an hour's drive from Port-au-Prince, and it is mediocre at that. Leclerc's appeal would seem to be to adults — perhaps to *consenting* adults — who are looking for a self-contained place of great luxury, charm, almost foolproof weather and high style. Leclerc is abundant in all of these.

18

Lucullan Pleasures
Are Where You Find Them

The Catalina Restaurant in the Bayous

You can eat in motel dining rooms along the Gulf coast of Alabama if you have no pride. The food will be pretty much what you would find in New Jersey. But eating in roadside cafés, diners and seafood restaurants on the end of decrepit bayou docks entitles you to hold up your head. Honorable mention goes to any out-of-state traveler who pulls up a chair to a table in a restaurant whose only sign outside reads EATS.

It was February, and I had found a fragile spot of sunshine on Dauphin Island, a thin spit of sand about thirty miles long that is connected to the mainland of Alabama by a bridge and a causeway. Purely on impulse, I had turned to the right, away from Fort Gaines, which lies at the eastern tip of the island, and I had driven all the way to the end. The island was almost deserted and as far as I could tell all the hotels were closed. I found a stretch of lowland that seemed hospitable to scrub pines and little else, and left my car on the side of the road. The beach there is a succession of magnificent dunes, and I burrowed between two of them to shelter me from the wind and turned my face up to the sun. It was a weak sun but it was welcome; I had encountered five straight days of cold rain. A mile or so to the east, a long dock extended into the Gulf of Mexico, and I could see some fishermen on the very end, but aside from them there was no one in sight. On the hottest days of summer, during July and August when the Alabama sun is at its fiercest, this strip of sand must be a fragment of hell, but right now the pale sun was glorious and lying there I was at peace with the world. Until I suddenly realized I was hungry. It was time for lunch; past time.

Hurrying back to Mobile through the marshland, I saw a sign pointing down an unpaved road to a place called Bayou La Batre. It didn't look promising; even the sign seemed to possess an apologetic air. But I had breakfasted in Mobile, and I wasn't overly anxious to return there for lunch. I turned down the road to Bayou La Batre.

The country was bleak and flat, and there were few houses. In fields of weeds, ancient automobiles resting on Nehi and Dr Pepper crates rusted· silently and forlorn. Most of the dwellings were summer fishing shacks, surrounded by pines and scrub growth, and all were touched with the decay of abandonment. Advertisements for snuff adorned the outbuildings. I gathered that Society Brand was the favorite, but Banjo was a comer. Pecan trees shaded a few of the shacks, and there was an occasional crepe myrtle, but mostly the landscape was relieved only by pines. It was incomparably ugly, and as I pushed farther along the road the sky became heavily overcast and a light rain started to fall. My hunger grew, and there was nothing to indicate whether Bayou La Batre was ten miles away or a hundred.

Some distance down the road I saw a man walking toward me. I flipped on the windshield wiper to make sure my imagination was not getting the upper hand. When I came abreast of him, I stopped and rolled down the window. He was wearing a baseball cap and a grin wide enough to expose two front teeth which, so far as I could see, were all that he possessed. I asked if I was anywhere near a place to eat. His grin widened to confirm my estimate. "You're mighty lucky," he replied. I waited, but he stood there as though the next move were up to me. The pause became awkward; sooner or later one of us would have to speak. "Why am I lucky?" I asked, breaking the strange silence. "Because," he said, "you're no more than half a mile from the best restaurant in Alabama *and* Louisiana. Anything you eat after that gonna make you think you camping out." He paused again and stared at me in silence. I asked if the restaurant had a name. "Catalina," he said. I thanked him and started to drive off. He held up his hand, and I stopped. "Don't look so good on the outside," he warned.

The Catalina appeared a few minutes later, and it looked dismal. Almost covered by an enormous live oak tree, it was a sprawling one-story brick building set back only a few feet from the shoulder of the road. A letter had long ago fallen from its sign, and it now read ESTAURANT. I parked my car, and went through the screen door, letting it bang behind me.

Drawing a picture of the Catalina Restaurant isn't easy, but I'll try. A cavernous dining room opened from a small entrance hall, which seemed to serve as an estuary leading to other rooms. The dining room contained possibly forty or fifty tables, and all were unadorned, rough, and accommodated four people. On top of each table was a huge bottle of catsup, several different brands of steak sauce, a bottle of Tabasco, and a large jar of salad dressing from a supermarket. I got the impression that the proprietor had found out what the customers wanted, and had supplied it in quantity. Bright overhead lights did away with any foolish thoughts of a romantic atmosphere. Apparently the customers were not to be pampered; one found an empty table and sat there. A middle-aged woman, carrying an empty tray, came to my table and, smiling affably, asked, "What'll it be?"

I said I'd start with a bloody mary. "Not here, you won't," she said. "No booze." Her gaze roamed the room, and my eyes followed hers. About half the tables were filled, and I suddenly realized that all the customers were men. "What you want to eat?" she asked, turning back to me.

I said I didn't know. "Have you a menu?" I asked.

"I can get you a menu," she said, "but there isn't all that much on it. I can tell you what we got."

I tried a new tack. "What do you recommend?" I asked.

"You like shrimp?" she inquired. I said that I did. "Okay," she said. "The shrimp's good. Buy them every day down the road at Bayou La Batre. Strictly fresh. How about a side of shrimp for starters?"

I asked how they were cooked, and she looked at me curiously. Obviously she had drawn a problem eater. An out-of-stater most likely. "Boiled," she said, "with a little Tabasco in the water to spice them up. I eat them myself, every day." The latter, I realized, was her ultimate reassurance. If that didn't clinch the deal, nothing would.

I settled for shrimps to begin with. "What after that?" I inquired. "I'm hungry."

She thought a moment. "How about the West Indies salad?"

I was back being a problem eater again. "What's that?" I wanted to know.

"You not from around here, are you?" she asked. Her worst suspicions were proving true. I said I was from New York, and she permitted her eyes to roll ceilingward. "West Indies salad is our specialty," she explained, keeping a steady grip on her patience. "Most all of these folks are eating it." She waved vaguely about the room. "It's fresh crabmeat marinated for fourteen hours."

"Marinated in what?" I asked.

"That's for me to know and you to find out," she replied tartly. There was a brief silence as we gazed at each other. "It's a secret," she said.

"Okay," I said. "I'll try it."

She started away, then turned back to me. "And to drink?" she inquired.

I said I'd settle for a beer.

"Not here you won't," she said. "No booze." Again we were at a standoff. I asked what she recommended, following a now-familiar path.

"Mr. Pibb," she said flatly. "I like Mr. Pibb. Or you can have ice tea."

I said I'd have a Mr. Pibb, but I couldn't put the force of much enthusiasm behind it.

"It goes good with West Indies salad," she reassured me. "You did the right thing." Then she was gone.

Service was fast. She was back almost instantly with a plate containing a mound of steaming shrimp that I could see at a glance was enough for not one but several people. She placed the plate in front of me, handed me several paper napkins, pointed to the various bottles on the table, and said: "If you don't see what you want, ask for it."

I peeled a shrimp and ate it, and I am prepared to depose under oath it was the finest shrimp I had ever tasted. It was fresh, tender, cooked just enough, and the Tabasco lent it a spicy taste that made shrimp sauce superfluous. I ate possibly half of them, and then pushed the plate aside. I had to give the West Indies salad a fair shake. The waitress passed and I stopped her. "What's the matter?" she asked, eyeing the plate. "Didn't like them?" I liked them fine, I said, but I was saving room for the main course. She nodded sagely and took the plate away.

The West Indies salad, when it was placed in front of me, left me with the suspicion that I should have quit with the shrimps when I was ahead. The chunks of crabmeat were gray, not white, and they floated in what appeared to be a sea of oil. "You can eat it out the bowl," the waitress said, "or spoon it out on your plate. Some like it one way, some the other. That's why I brought you a plate. Now I'll get you your Mr. Pibb."

I decided to get the crabmeat out of the oil with all possible speed; fourteen hours was enough. I scooped up a spoonful, let it drain against the edge of the bowl, and deposited it on my plate, where it looked no more appealing than it had afloat. I tasted it tentatively. Wonderful is a tricky and imprecise word to employ in describing food, but before I get into specifics I want to put the word wonderful on the record. The crabmeat, despite its appearance, was firm and fresh, lime juice or lemon juice imparted a tart taste, and some unidentified spices gave it a flavor unlike anything I had known before. I settled down to it happily.

The waitress looked at me approvingly when she brought the Mr. Pibb. Out-of-staters were often crazy,

God knows, but they recognized good food when they found it. She obviously enjoyed seeing a man relish what he ate. "Most folks drink Mr. Pibb out of the bottle," she said. "You want a glass I'll get you one." I shook my head; my mouth was full.

I ate all of the West Indies salad. And I drank some of the Mr. Pibb. I sat there, in the Catalina Restaurant, for nearly half an hour after I finished eating, too satisfied to move. Then I paid the check, which was a little less than three dollars, and walked out through the entrance hall to the screen door. "Come again, you hear," the waitress had said when she took my money. It was raining hard now, and I ran from the door to my car. I started the motor and turned on the windshield wiper. The waitress's words rang in my ears. I would come again, I decided, come hell or Hiawatha, as an aunt of mine who read too much used to say.

Dinner with the Big Boys

THE most sensitive and cultivated palates in New York, a sometimes questionable center of civilization and sophistication, are said to belong to the forty-nine members of the Lucullus Circle, a publicity-shy group of gourmets' gourmets that meets four times a year for a feast that can only be described as, well, Lucullan. The reader notes, I trust, my *assumption* that these forty-nine eaters are the most discerning diners in town, since comparisons are tricky and it is impossible to say positively that this person appreciates fine food and wine more than that person. A further complicating element in the gourmet picture is that once past a certain level in eating, a stage where the diner moves from simple eating to eating *con molta passione*, a bit of theater enters to cloud the issue somewhat and make it difficult to distinguish the truly sophisticated palate from that of the pretender.

I knew a man who imagined himself to be a gourmet, and he put so much time and effort into it that the poor fellow couldn't enjoy anything he ate. Roast beef hash in a roadside diner was enough to cause him to pause at the cash register, select a toothpick, and recall for the cashier some other great roast beef hashes he had encountered in his travels.

Unfortunately, his viscera had all of the sensitivity of an incinerator, and where wine was concerned, in a blindfold test he couldn't distinguish a Bordeaux from Kool-Aid; yet he persisted in playing the role he had selected for himself. All wine he invested with human behavior or personality traits, and I once shook my head in disbelief when I heard him sadly remark that a bottle of inexpensive California wine had been "smothered in infancy." Oscar Wilde once wrote, "To be natural is such a very difficult pose to keep up," and, as was so often the case, Wilde knew what he was talking about. I yearned desperately for the courage to suggest to my friend that he seek social salvation along avenues he was better equipped to explore, but this called for bravery that bordered on sheer recklessness and I never rose to the occasion.

Memories of my friend were enough to dwarf but they could not dispel my excitement when I discovered in my mail a handsome invitation to attend, as a guest, a Lucullus Circle dinner. I accepted with what I later feared may have been construed as indecent haste, but in the small New England village in which I live one isn't summoned to such functions every day. The dinner was to be in a private dining room on the fourth floor of the Waldorf-Astoria Hotel, it was a black-tie affair, and I was forewarned that no cocktails or hard drinks would be served. This, of course, was to prevent one's taste apparatus from being anesthetized.

I arrived promptly at seven, according to instructions, and found a half-dozen other guests milling about a large table situated in the center of the vestibule leading to the dining room. The guests looked well-to-do. There were four large silver soup bowls on the table together with five opened bottles of wine. My host welcomed me warmly and pointed to the table. "The soups are *les amuse-bouche*," he explained, "and we have those here before we enter the dining room. They are four authentic regional American winter soups — Key West turtle soup, Louisiana gumbo, borscht from Pennsylvania, and a cream of corn soup from the Carolinas. The wines are selected to go with the soups, and I suggest you try them all." He left me to greet some other arrivals, and I moved cautiously to the table. The wines were Château de Bellevue Morgon 1973, Cabernet Sauvignon 1971, Anjou Rosé 1974, Château la Haute Graviere 1971, and Pinot Chardonnay 1973.

I accepted a bowl of cream of corn soup, and was studying the wines when a tall man with a mustache, noting my choice of soup, said, "You've made a good selection. I've tried them all and that's the best. Incidentally, go easy on the wines out here. There will be at least twelve with dinner." I thanked him and took a glass of Château la Haute Graviere. Both the soup and the wine were excellent. Things were off to a good start.

When we entered the dining room a short time later, I saw a large oval table banked with flowers and candelabra. There were twelve wine glasses at each plate, and two brandy glasses. The *escriteau*, or menu for the evening, together with a card listing the wines, was printed in

French and placed at each setting. I saw at a glance that there were six main courses together with an *intermède*, a sherbet served in the middle of the meal to rest and refresh the stomach before one proceeded to further excesses. (I thought of the vomitorium which in ancient days served the same purpose, less delicately, for Roman feasts.) There were two wines with each course, and Camus Napoleon brandy and Rieder William pear brandy to accompany the coffee. I wondered if I could go the route.

The waiters, for the occasion, showed no inclination to maintain normal standards of insolence and lethargy, yet it was almost midnight when the dinner was finished and cigars were passed. The chef and sous-chef were brought in, introduced, and given seats and brandy. My host arose and named one member of the Circle to criticize the meal and another one to criticize the wines. I settled back, interested to see how serious the criticism would be. The chef, I noticed, was totally relaxed, sipping his brandy, but the sous-chef, a much younger man, looked uneasy and gazed around the table in silent reproach at what he feared was to come.

The critic of the meal was George Nelson, who was identified to me as a financier in Wall Street, and he was obviously relishing his role. A man of medium build and very fair skin, he smiled graciously as he looked about the room. "This is one of the best dinners I have ever attended here," he began. "The soups, in the outer room, were an amusing change, and I think we need more surprises like that. So far as the dinner was concerned, the first course, the turtle, was a little heavy, but superb. Then came the carp, which" – he paused – "well, was perhaps a bit too ambitious. The fennel, with which it was poached, is very famous in France, as we all know, where it is used in this manner with *loup de mer*, but it worked well, *extremely* well, with the carp, and was perhaps its salvation. I must say I was surprised." He glanced at the chef, who nodded slightly in agreement.

"Now we come to the roast veal," he continued. "The veal in this country cannot be compared with French veal, but this was probably the best American veal I have ever tasted. The Granite au Marc de Bourgogne du Marquis d'Angerville is not to be discussed as it was served only to clear the palate and for no other purpose. Then there was the *mousse de jambon de Virginie*. This concept was a bit" — he paused again, then found the word for which he was searching — "a bit heavy, especially after what we had already eaten. It was really gilding the lily, and I think we would have been better served if we had had something a good bit lighter. The Brie was *courant*, in fact much too *courant*, and the dessert — the *crêpes soufflées aux pralines* — was too much. Something —" again he searched his mind — "something more *innocent* would have done as well. But my overall conclusion is that it was an extraordinary meal." He smiled at the chef and the sous-chef and took his seat.

The wine was to be criticized by Leonard S. Sharif, a dignified man in his sixties who held the wine card in his hand for reference. "I agree with my friend, George Nelson, in regard to the food," Mr. Sharif began, "but I must be less kind to the wines. The two California wines served with the first course — the Petit Sirah 'York Creek' 1973 and the Zinfandel 'Clos du Val' 1972 — were outstanding examples of California wines. Right now they compare favorably with small French wines, but how will they be twenty years from now? I wonder. The Sirah showed up well tonight, but the Zinfandel was the more interesting wine. There is a theory that Zinfandel originally came from Hungary, but its origins are something of a mystery. I have always felt that Zinfandel is the Beaujolais of California. If I had to choose between the Sirah and the Zinfandel, I would say positively that the Zinfandel was the more sophisticated of the two wines." There was a general nodding of agreement among the guests.

"The two white Burgundies with the second course," he continued, "were pleasant to drink, but I felt a decided preference for the Puligny-Montrachet 1972. It had an infinitely better breeding than the Meursault Casse-Tete 1973. While they were both pleasant, this is not to say that either was a *big* wine. The Château Branaire Ducru 1955, served with the veal, is not a very well known wine but I think we all must agree that tonight it was in fine fettle!" There was a ripple of applause, but whether for the wine or for the critic's perception, I couldn't tell. "It came from 1955," he went on, "which we all know was an excellent year, and it made the Château Haut Brion 1959 taste like water. The Haut Brion still has a long, long way to go. Tonight it just wasn't ready."

Mr. Sharif paused as though he expected some rebuttal, but when none materialized, he continued: "On the fourth course — the ham mousse — the wine and the food came completely apart. Neither the Château Montrose 1959 nor the Château Latour 1954 was exactly right for the dish, but I wonder if *any* wine goes well with ham. I don't think so. The Latour 1954 was no good at all, and the Montrose was no better, which makes me wonder if one is better off with a cru of a poor year or a good vineyard. Neither of these wines was up to the standards of those that preceded them." If this was an unpopular opinion, it was taken in silence.

"The two Burgundies which accompanied the cheese," he continued, glancing at his card to refresh his memory, "were, in a way, disappointing. The Vosne Romanée 1971 is a district wine. It is just from an area and is not a vineyard wine. Nor do I rate the Nuits Saint Georges 1971 much above the Romanée, the latter of which at least shows some signs of future greatness once it matures. I had the feeling that the Saint Georges is going through second fermentation, and tonight, I must insist, it was not a drinkable wine." I was sorry to hear this because I had enjoyed the Saint Georges and had even made the terrible mistake of calling my seatmate's attention to it, but of course this only makes the value of an expert's opinion abundantly clear. It keeps you from enjoying a wine you might enjoy by mistake.

"Let us move on to the Sauternes that were served with the crêpes," Mr. Sharif said. "The Château d'Yquem 1958 suffered from the fact that it was a bad year. A good year for d'Yquem was 1971. The d'Yquem we had tonight was not what a d'Yquem ought to be, nor, for that matter, was the Château Rieussec 1971."

Mr. Sharif sat down solemnly, and a member of the Circle arose. "I'd like to add one thing to what Mr. Sharif has said," he asserted. "The d'Yquem was not an exciting wine. I wouldn't want to take it to bed with me."

That ended the dinner. As I went out I was handed, as a gift, a magnum of Château Simard 1971, Grand Cru de Saint Emilion, Château Bottled. I got in a cab with the magnum cradled in the crook of my arm. I liked eating with the big boys.

19

A Haunted Place

IT was a Saturday evening. Bali, like all the other tropical islands in the Indian Ocean, is occasionally afflicted with rain. The weather for a week or more had been superb, though fairly hot, but it had clouded up early in the afternoon and by nightfall it was raining gently but steadily. The driver, who was to take me to the village of Mas to have dinner at the home of Bali's leading artist, drove slowly through the rain, taking care, it seemed, not to splatter the bicyclists who made an endless chain in the pitch blackness at the edge of the road. There is something almost narcotic about a gentle, tropical rain, and a half-hour later when he turned from the main road into the private drive of the artist's compound, I awoke from a sound sleep. Peering through the rain and darkness, I saw two immense carved stone columns and what appeared to be four or five pavilions with lighted verandahs, grouped around a large open area. My host, who was seated on the verandah of one of the pavilions, greeted me affably and indicated with a gesture toward a formally laid table that we were to eat immediately.

I ate heartily, as I always do in Bali because there are so

many different dishes, and each one is novel and surprising and almost invariably delicious, but the entire evening had a dreamlike quality that I now know is something especially Balinese since so many of my recollections of that island possess the same quality. I recall the quietness within the compound, the moist warmth of the evening, the dripping of the rain, and the ghostly sight of a waiter walking up the driveway carrying a tray of hot dishes while a companion carried an open umbrella to keep rain from falling on the food. Fifty yards away, two children were playing on the porch of another pavilion while an elderly woman sewed, and I asked my host if the children were his. He smiled and said that they were. The woman wasn't mentioned, but this, too, was Balinese.

There's a rumor — I'm starting it now — that Bali is something very close to being one of the last genuine tourist paradises on earth, and while paradise is a difficult word to write down seriously on paper, there is much truth to it. Physically, it is one of the most beautiful places I have ever seen, with trees and plants so luxuriantly and magnificently green that at first glance one can see little else; rice terraces draining artfully from high to low but so gradually that the fall must be calibrated in fractions of inches; volcanic peaks whose slopes are as green as jungles; flowering trees and carved stone temples everywhere; and above it all a dazzling sun in a blue sky. But as though discontented with the natural beauty, the Balinese have applied their own colors to the canvas, the brilliant magenta, yellow, blue and pink of their clothes, the golden brown hue of their bodies, and the wild mixture of colors in the fruit and vegetables they carry. In Bali, the eye is under constant and violent assault.

"This is a haunted place," said Mr. Oka. "We believe in

spirits." Mr. Oka was my friend and guide, and he believed in spirits as matter-of-factly as a Texan believes in Dallas. It was my first day in Bali, and we had paused under a tree from a branch of which hung a small bundle of fruit and grain. "This is an offering for safe passage," he said. When I demanded to know who put it there, he shrugged his shoulders. "What difference does it make?" he asked. "We live here as we did four thousand years ago. There are hundreds of offerings, thousands perhaps, being set out in Bali today. Some are to protect the new rice crops that have just been planted, some are offerings in temples, some are set at the foot of banyan trees, which are sacred, some are — like this — to ask safety for passersby. The offerings are tokens of respect and gratitude."

Mr. Oka was right; in the days that followed I saw hundreds of offerings. One day I asked him to stop the car when I saw a group of people standing in a rice paddy beside a strange object. Walking on the raised dikes between the tiny canals, and occasionally jumping from dike to dike, I reached the group and saw that it was a farmer and his neighbors offering food and flowers to a deity in the hope that the new crop would be blessed. They permitted me to join them with curiosity but no disfavor. A few days later when I pointed out to Mr. Oka some long plastic shreds hanging from a pole in a rice paddy and told him it was the first plastic offering I had seen, he smiled and shook his head. "That's to frighten the birds," he said.

In the small corner of life that Bali occupies there are few of the disruptive results of a society undergoing industrialization, or even a feeling that the old knowledge has become less relevant. To the Balinese, nothing changes, and the traditional knowledge is always relevant. This makes for something both majestic and simple, something never terribly complicated, but yet vastly impressive. In the raw heat of noon one day I wandered into a family compound. Inside there was shade from palm and frangipani trees, and some small children were playing beneath a huge mango tree. In the house temple, the priest was embroidering a piece of cloth; when he saw me he bowed low, then turned his gaze immediately back to his work. Carved stone gods sat about in what appeared to be small cages, with offerings of flowers and bamboo strips strewn in front of them. Villagers and children lounged in the shade, and an elderly woman trudged through the compound carrying a basket on her head. She was naked above the waist, her spent breasts drooped, and she looked through me without seeing. A baby girl strolled nonchalantly naked behind her, her tiny bottom covered with dust from sitting on the ground. The compound slumbered, its spirit a pleasing blend of tranquillity, timelessness and brotherhood.

One day I came upon a man repairing a bicycle tire beside the road. His little daughter was busily engaged in picking some roadside flowers and arranging a small offering beneath the naked wheel. The purpose was to speed and make permanent the repair, and I have no doubt that it helped.

I have spoken already of Balinese food, but I want to mention a restaurant that is called Puri Suling and is about six miles from Sanur, the main beach resort. I am tempted to say that it is in a jungle, because that is the way it seemed to me, but the Balinese would doubtless laugh at that. Anyway, you approach it by a long path that winds through foliage that is almost overwhelming. Once around a bend and out of sight of the road you pause to strike an enormous gong to announce your arrival. A young Balinese girl hastens up the path and leads you to the restaurant, which is a covered verandah on the side of a steep hill. At the foot of the hill runs a small river, and across the narrow valley, on the other slope, is a palm-thatched structure sheltering a half-dozen musicians who entertain the diners with a concert of rather haunting music played on bamboo wind instruments. The waitresses, and they seemed to be as many as the diners, were dressed in lime-green silk tunics, tight belts, and batik shirts. All were barefoot, all had frangipani blossoms in their hair, all had wide, innocent eyes, and without a second's hesitation I would swear they were among the most beautiful creatures in the world. And now, belatedly, a word about the food. I began with *soto Madura,* an excellent soup, and went on to grilled tuna steak, a subtly flavored shrimp pastry, the ever-present rice, and seven totally indescribable dishes variously served with peanuts, onions and fiery sauces. I have not the slightest idea what they were, but all were excellent. Dessert consisted of banana fritters with shredded coconut.

Outside of Denpasar and the larger villages, life in Bali is lived in what at times is almost a continuous roadside community. Traffic is mostly by bicycle or on foot, although the automobile intrudes more each year. Houses are often situated back from the road, but commerce — oh, what glorious commerce! — thrives in tiny grass-roofed shelters only inches from it. There are fruit stands heaped with all of the wanton extravagance of the tropics, including some strange things I not only had never before seen but had not even heard of. Some stands sold only canned goods, some offered only straw and woven objects, and some were piled with fabrics so colorful as to seem almost aflame. The roads were thronged with people, ducks, dogs, pigs and chickens, all seeming to know exactly where they were going and for what purpose. One day I saw five children riding one bi-

cycle, and another day I came across a little boy of about
five carrying his baby sister, very gently, on his back. It
was a tender and moving sight, and I shall not forget it.

Mr. Oka had mentioned the word *barong* to me a number of times, and finally I asked him what it was. A barong,
it turns out, is the effigy of a mythical monster that is also a
kind of deity. When a barong needs to be moved, for any
reason, it is the cause of a tremendous procession, for
which every Balinese who hears of it will drop what he or
she is doing in order to participate. I heard that a new
barong had just been completed and was to be transported
five miles away to the scene of its permanent shrine, and I
sought out Mr. Oka to see if he would help me find it.
Finding a barong procession, it turned out, is about as difficult as finding a sunrise; it's hard not to find it. This one
was so spectacular as to wring an expression of admiration
even from Mr. Oka, who I gathered had seen just about
everything Bali had to offer. There was music, there were
costumes, and there were marchers by the hundreds. The
procession moved down the road, skirted a rice paddy and
disappeared, but long after it was gone from sight I could
hear the singing and the music.

The rainy season in Bali begins in October and extends
through March, and during that period it can be counted
on to rain at least a short while every day. During the dry
season the streams may dry up, but seepage from the
mountain lakes keeps the island green. There are two rice
crops a year and sometimes, in a good year, three. This is
why, from the air, the rice paddies give a checkerboard
effect. They appear emerald green, lime green, apple green,
chartreuse and brown, depending upon the stage of growth
of each field.

Bali exerts a strange spell. How can I forget the night I

sat in a wooden chair in an open field and watched a fire-walker, deep in a trance, tread on a bed of glowing embers? I examined the soles of his feet carefully while his companions were seeking to awaken him, and there was no evidence of burns. Or the morning that I attended a tooth-filing ceremony, in which two young maidens — upon reaching the proper age — had their teeth filed manually until all were even, even though the pain must have been considerable? Or dining at twilight in the garden of Mr. Oka's home while a musician, stationed out of sight behind a wall, provided a mournful serenade on a flute, and bamboo shreds fluttered in the evening breeze?

Mr. Oka said Bali was a haunted place, and I think he's right. But it is a lovely place and a fragile place and I feel a great need to protect it. On my last day I was lunching outdoors and a butterfly flew in and settled gently on the papaya on my plate. It drank thirstily, thanked me inaudibly, and sailed away. I last saw it fluttering in a hibiscus hedge. I suppose it could happen anywhere, but I can't think of Bali without thinking of that lunch and that butterfly and that hibiscus hedge.

20

Twelve Hours to *Anywhere*

His body was a historical record of past indulgences and one could tell at a glance that his sense of importance would never collide with his sense of humor. He accepted a glass of champagne from the steward in the waiting room as though he were doing the former a favor, then turned to me and raised the glass aloft. "It's an historic occasion," he said in heavily accented English, and I half expected him to click his heels. "Very few people have flown as fast as we are to fly today." I took a glass of champagne and raised it toward him. There was bound to be an adventurer on the first scheduled flight of the Concorde from Paris to Rio, and his credentials seemed flawless, from the casual silk scarf around the neck to the navy blazer and houndstooth trousers.

I had heard that the most surprising thing about the Concorde was that there was nothing really surprising about it. It flew very high and it flew very fast, but as an exciting experience it was said to lack the high drama that accompanied the last step forward in civil aviation — the escalation to jet travel by a public that had become bored with the previous generation of lumbering piston aircraft. Still, there was a noticeable air of expectancy among the group assembled in the Concorde departure lounge at Charles de Gaulle Airport awaiting the takeoff of Air France Flight 085 to São Paulo, Brazil. There was good reason: the Concorde had made only a few flights on its South American run on an experimental basis, it *was* a novelty, it flew at twice the speed of sound at an altitude eleven miles above the earth, there had been a tremendous amount written about it, and it had overnight become the storm center of a violent controversy over landing rights in the United States. And who, outside of the military, had traveled at speeds greater than those made by sounds?

When the announcement to board was called, the adventurer took one final glass of champagne, emptied it quickly, tucked a copy of *Le Monde* under his arm, picked up a small black attaché case, the kind seen under the arm of every German businessman in Europe, and strode purposefully aboard, his spirits afloat on wings of imaginary applause. I admired him but I wasn't sure why; perhaps theater appeals to us all.

The plane was not nearly as large as I had imagined it would be; it is a rather small aircraft, a fact that strikes one forcibly upon entering. The interior of the cabin is only about eight feet wide and six and one-half feet high, giving the impression of being a long, narrow tube, which is pretty much what it is. There are no wings in the conventional sense but the plane possesses a deltoid formation well toward the rear that is said to provide high maneuverability at low speeds. I don't know what low speeds mean to a plane that cruises along at 1,350 miles per hour.

The Concorde is divided into two cabins, although there is only one class of service, and there are two seats on either side of a narrow aisle. On the right-hand side of the front wall of each cabin is a digital speed indicator called a mach-meter, which registers the air speed of the plane in terms of both subsonic and supersonic speed. The speed indicator exercised an almost total fascination on the passengers to the exclusion of everything else. Once the plane was off the ground, in a takeoff that seemed to differ from a conventional plane in no respect whatever, I found that I could not keep my eyes off the thing. Nothing short of a crash landing could have torn my eyes from the machmeter. In about three minutes of flight, we registered Mach 0.50 or one-half the speed of sound and after five minutes we touched Mach 0.93. For the next twenty minutes nothing else happened, the speed fluctuated between Mach 0.92 and Mach 0.94. We passed the coast of Europe before we passed the sound barrier. A stewardess was passing out headsets, and when she moved out of my path of vision I saw that we had gone to Mach 1.02 and that I was traveling faster than I had ever moved in my entire lifetime. There was no sensation whatever in moving ahead of sound. I drank a glass of champagne but I was not sure what I was toasting.

It was forty-three minutes later that we touched Mach 2.00, or twice the speed of sound, and by then I was aware that we were going like a bat out of hell. It was an odd sensation and one difficult to describe but the feel of great forward thrust was impossible to ignore. Moreover, a loud whine had developed, not enough to make conversation impossible but loud enough to sometimes drown out the captain's announcements from the flight deck.

Conventional planes — 747's and 707's — seldom if ever fly above 35,000 feet; the Concorde, when it is pouring it on, cruises at 60,000 feet with the cabin pressurized to the equivalent of about 5,500 feet, which involves no more discomfort than one would encounter in the city of Denver. From that height, the captain said, one could see the curvature of the earth. I could see only clouds but I was perfectly willing to believe him. The air temperature at this altitude is around −76 degrees Fahrenheit, which I suppose is something of a help in cooling the skin of the plane, whose wing edges at Mach 2.00 reach temperatures of 347 degrees. However, the development of aluminum alloys capable of maintaining their strength at these temperatures is what guarantees that the aircraft doesn't turn into a cinder. The Concorde, in its over-ocean cruising, moves along at Mach 2.02 or 2.03. To go much faster than that, new alloys would be required, so the outer limit of the Concorde's speed is definitely established.

Although Air France Flight 085 is described as Paris to São Paulo, the Concorde portion ends at Rio de Janeiro, and passengers connect with a conventional plane for the final leg of the flight. Because of the need to refuel, the Concorde lands briefly at Dakar, on the bulge of West Africa, and shortly before arrival it drops to subsonic speed. Unlike Paris, where passengers boarded the plane without being able to see it, at Dakar we descended to the tarmac, and for most of us it was the first glimpse we had had of the exterior of the craft. There was an immediate flurry of photographing. The adventurer, who was now mopping his forehead with the silk scarf, asked if I would take his photograph standing directly under the drooping nose of the plane. I agreed, but his demands escalated. He posed in every conceivable posture, the most dramatic, I thought, being the fraudulent bit of business where he was waving to an imaginary group at the airport that had presumably come to welcome him. As we walked to the terminal building, I saw he was wilting badly from the heat.

"Rio will be cooler than this, won't it?" he asked appealingly. I assured him it would be.

Shortly before arrival in Dakar we had been served lunch, which Air France apologetically explained as a "modification" of its service on long-haul aircraft because the Concorde cabin staff had at its disposal only two hours for this task. So far as I was concerned no apology was necessary. There was an excellent caviar pastry, smoked salmon, and a variety of hors d'oeuvres, followed by *caille chevassu* (quail), *homard Thermidor* (lobster), *riz pilaw, pointes d'asperges, gâteau Mignon,* and *fraises au sucre.* The strawberries were ripe, the cake was excellent, and the asparagus was tender. With it was served Taittinger champagne, a fine Burgundy (Hospices de Beaune 1969), a Médoc (Château Pichon Lalande 1970), and a variety of liqueurs. Apologies indeed!

After taking off from Dakar, the plane headed southwest across the South Atlantic Ocean, and we went quickly to Mach 2.04. By this time the machmeter had lost most of its fascination, and the passengers were reading, listening to their headsets, napping, or otherwise behaving as on a conventional plane. Tea and pastries were served, and a short time later the captain announced that he was preparing to descend to Rio. As the plane taxied to the gate, the captain reported that our actual flying time from Paris to Rio — deducting ground time in Dakar — had been five hours and forty-five minutes. It was hard to believe.

In the space of a few hours I had been on three continents — Europe, Africa, and South America — and I had traveled at a speed that would have delivered me to the most remote spot in the world in twelve hours. From Paris to Rio would have taken almost twelve hours in the fastest subsonic plane now flying. Disembarking at Rio from the

Concorde I had no feeling of exhaustion, since the human body is not affected by speed (a fortunate circumstance when one realizes that the earth revolves around the sun at an average speed of 62,000 miles per hour). In Paris, an Air France official had shown me around the luxurious Concorde lounges and explained that every effort was being made to speed up check-in and ground services so that the time gained in the air would not be lost to passengers by ground delays. A Concorde passenger could be deposited by taxi at the entrance to Charles de Gaulle Airport *twelve minutes before takeoff time* and get aboard the plane comfortably. Such split-second timing isn't encouraged, mind you, but suggests the extent to which the entire Concorde performance is geared to speed.

I will not dwell excessively on the controversy now swirling around the plane's planned introduction of service to American cities. The scheduled flying time westbound to Dulles, outside Washington, will be three hours and fifty minutes as opposed to eight hours and twenty-five minutes for 707's and seven hours and fifty-five minutes for 747's. The fare now contemplated will be the present first-class rate plus a 20 percent SST surcharge. Much of the opposition to the Concorde, I note, is based upon anxiety over environmental impact, although this anxiety seems strangely lacking toward the thousands of supersonic military planes that are criss-crossing the skies of the United States all day and all night. Where airport noise is concerned, the Concorde is noisier than the DC-10 or the Tristar but no more so than the 707. Sonic boom is hardly a matter of consideration, since the Concorde does not fly at supersonic speed within one hundred miles of either coast. But regardless of how political and environmental winds are now blowing, there seems very little doubt that the supersonic transport is the next generation of commercial planes, whether it is the Concorde or some modification of the Concorde. Perhaps what I am really saying is that the Concorde is the plane of the future and it has now arrived.

There was a large welcoming crowd at the Rio airport, and it took some time for me to work my way through it. As my baggage was being loaded in the back of the taxi, a familiar face appeared at the window. The scarf had disappeared and the blazer was folded under an arm. "If you're going toward the Copacabana area," he said, "perhaps you would oblige me by sharing your cab." I motioned for him to get in, and we started through the maze of traffic. He gave me a beguiling smile. "The fact is," he said, "I couldn't afford to take this trip, and in another sense I couldn't afford to miss it. Do you know what I mean?" I said that I did, and he leaned forward to roll down the window. "It's quite as warm here as at Dakar," he said. He was perspiring wildly, and his hand moved to his hip pocket. But instead of bringing forth the silk scarf, he produced a heavy napkin, in one corner of which was printed AIR FRANCE.

21

Adam, Eve and "Le Minimum"

If a blind man were put ashore on the Ile du Levant, a rocky island in the Mediterranean a few miles from the French Riviera, he would find very little that was distinctive about it. He would smell the odor of lavender and pine, there would be rocks beneath his feet everywhere, and he would hear the sound of people laughing and talking and splashing in the sea. But if his sight were suddenly restored he would probably buckle at the knees at what he saw. Specifically, he would see — depending upon the time of the year — perhaps as many as several thousand stark-naked men, women and children acting as though it were the most natural thing in the world to go without clothes. The Ile du Levant is very likely the world's most famous nudist refuge.

Nudism is an old-fashioned word and one that brings to mind the image of overweight couples playing volleyball at a tacky camp in the pine barrens of New Jersey, but if there is a more fashionable word for going without clothes it escapes me at the moment. At Tahiti Plage, the uninhibited end of the beach at Saint-Tropez, girls for the past few summers have been discarding their tops, and a few German resorts on the North Sea have relaxed their rules about beach attire, and even in the Caribbean — most notably the French island of Guadalupe — there are a few beaches where nakedness is permitted. But the Ile du Levant is to nudity what Saint Moritz is to skiing, a fashionable resort where one can encounter attractive people from all over Europe who have congregated on a scenically appealing island with only one thing on their minds and nothing — practically nothing at all — on their bodies. Protestations of physical fitness and health as motivations for nakedness have, like volleyball, faded into history; *erotisme* is the appeal, and the new sexual candor allows its acknowledgment.

No membership in any organization is required at Ile du Levant, there are no entry restrictions, there are no tests to pass and no forms to fill out. One simply takes a boat to the island — most visitors pack lightly — and once there, one may either join the undressed crowd or remain completely dressed, depending upon personal taste and inclination. That's almost true but not entirely. If the visitor goes to the beach — and there is only one — he or she must remove *all* clothing. But elsewhere on the island and especially in the village of Heliopolis, one wears what is called *le minimum*, which for both sexes is an inconsequential fragment of cloth that would make a G-string look like a caftan.

A large part of the island is a French naval base, an installation surrounded by a formidable wire fence bearing signs that say TERRAIN MILITAIRE. Whether the fence is to keep sailors in, or the nudists out, I can't say. Perhaps both. During the time I was on the island I saw no evidence of any activity at the naval base, but it can be truthfully said that my attention was elsewhere.

It's easy to find one's way around the Ile du Levant because there is so little of it. Aside from the naval base, there are a few rocky paths around the edge of the sea and some secluded coves sought out by those whose ambition goes beyond just sunning and swimming, a few dusty roads, a dock for the boats, some villas scattered among the pines and, of course, the town of Heliopolis, which lies at the summit of a steep hill. I arrived on the island early on the morning of a day near the end of summer, having taken a boat from Le Lavandou, and was somewhat relieved to find the dock completely deserted. I don't know what I expected, but I welcomed a brief period of decompression before plunging into the world of public nakedness. Nudity, I gather, is no longer an emotive word, and those who practice it feel no more the obligation to refer to themselves as naturists. I guess that's a step in the right direction, but I'm not sure.

Two other passengers had disembarked with me from the *Ile Enchantée*, a grubby boat that had vibrated badly during the entire crossing. One was a middle-aged man in corduroy shorts who clutched a *Guide Michelin* under his arm with the fervor of an evangelist clutching the Bible; the other was a bearded young man in sandals whose shirt was fastened low by a single button in what I took to be carefully studied nonchalance. Both of them disappeared ashore while the boat was being tied up and I never saw them again, or at least not that I know of. Under the circumstances it's hard to tell.

Carrying two heavy bags, I started climbing the hill to the village on the summit. It was a hellish climb; the road was dusty and the sun was hot. Loose rocks made the footing difficult, and my trench coat kept slipping from my shoulder where it rested precariously. I was exhausted when I reached the small square around which were clustered several small hotels and pensions, a bakeshop with a beaded entrance, some souvenir and novelty shops, and a garden restaurant. What I took to be the leading hotel, La Pomme d'Adam, had a *fermature annuelle* sign on the door, indicating it was closed for a seasonal holiday, so I walked across the dusty street to the garden restaurant and sank gratefully into a chair. It was still early and no other tables were occupied. A naked waiter came and asked if I would care to order. I asked for tea and croissants, which he promptly brought. Shortly after I started eating, a pretty, blond girl, wearing only sunglasses and *le minimum*, came out of the hotel beside the garden and took a table. She stared at me curiously, and I suddenly realized I must have looked strange dressed in a suit. To ease the situation, I removed my jacket and loosened my tie; I hoped she would consider this a token of intent. By the time I had finished eating, most of the tables were occupied.

I paid the check and went into the lobby of the Hotel Adam and Eve, of which the garden seemed to be a part, and I found a naked girl behind the desk. I said that I had no reservation but would like a room for a few days, and she selected a key and asked me to follow her. Following a naked lady, whom one has just met, is not as easy as it sounds; the eyes have a way of acting independent of the will. She led me outside, walked the length of a long porch, and open a door. "*Ça va?*" she asked, standing aside to let me see the room. I said it was satisfactory, and she said she would have my bags brought in right away. The room was shabbily furnished, but adequate; the bed was firm and the towels were clean. At the moment that seemed enough.

The window of my room was open, and through it I had a glimpse of a terrace and a garden beneath me, then the

ground shelved sharply into the slope that I had so labori-
ously climbed. Far below I could see into the tops of euca-
lyptus trees, and in the distance the blue of the sea. It was a
typical Mediterranean landscape; I had seen its equal often
in France, in Italy, in Greece, and in Cyprus. I unpacked,
and then walked across the street to a novelty shop, where
I bought a pair of espadrilles, a two-day-old copy of the
Paris edition of the *Herald-Tribune*, and *le minimum*. The
latter I stuffed into my pocket; I wasn't sure yet that I
would get up the nerve to wear it.

Back in my room, I put on white slacks, a shirt, and the
espadrilles, and started for the beach. It seemed odd leaving
my swimming trunks behind; it was like heading for a tennis court without a racket. The road to the beach passed
the boat dock and became a narrow, rocky path that clung
to the hillside above the sea. The beach, a small cove hidden
by pines, suddenly appeared below me. A path led down to
the sea, and beside the path was a sign that said: "*Visiteurs
— Adoptez les usages et les costumes des naturistes. Vous
serez les bienvenues.*" This separated the adventurous from
the timorous; beyond this point no clothes of any kind
were to be worn.

There were several hundred people on the beach when I
arrived at the cove, including a number of children. But for
the lack of clothes, the scene would have been no different
on any other beach on a languid September afternoon.
Two elderly English couples were playing bridge on a
copy of the *London Times*, an attractive redheaded woman
and her escort were leisurely eating lunch and passing a
bottle of wine back and forth, a stout Frenchman was hand-
pumping an inflatable raft, and an artist was making a charcoal sketch of his date — a statuesque young woman whose
breasts had been sunburned to a vivid crimson color. It

would be untrue to say there was no embarrassment; two teen-age girls came on the beach, giggling furiously and blushing. They dropped their towels and raced into the water.

I had always imagined that a naked society, because of the obvious temptations engendered, would energetically seek to erect a façade of Victorian respectability, but I found none of this on the Ile du Levant. On the contrary, there was evidence on all sides that sex was the reason that most of the people — most? — had come to the island and there was no compelling reason to ignore it. At least, the air was clear.

Many who arrive on the morning boat and return in the afternoon are plainly voyeurs out for a day's entertainment. They are ill at ease and, more often than not, shifty-eyed. Oddly — and this is perhaps why one day is enough for many people — mass nudity is more often comic than erotic. The nude body seldom falls into graceful positions, there aren't many people with truly fine bodies, and too often one encounters some droll incongruity, such as a ridiculous hat or a T-shirt with no trousers, that effectively derails any erotic train of thought.

Walking back up the hill later that day, I noticed a group of children playing in the rear of a small villa and was surprised to see that they were all wearing shorts and shirts. They struck me as being the only totally unselfconscious people I saw on the island.

Evenings on the island were dull. Sweaters appeared after dark when the evening air turned cool, people strolled around the tiny square buying postcards, and some dancing and card games developed in the garden. There was a nightclub in the village, a small place called La Caravelle, which featured striptease shows, three times a night. I didn't go and I would be inclined to disbelieve the kind of performances given, except that I saw the sign.

Two days later the sky was overcast and the weather was uncomfortably cool, and I left on the late-afternoon boat. There were six other passengers on the *Ile Enchantée*, all women and all dressed. They looked good. As the island slipped astern, a story of Victor Borge's flashed into my mind. Borge's young son had been to a swimming-pool birthday party, and when he came home his father sought to find out what had happened. Under questioning, the boy said that he had had a good time, that he had been swimming, and that there had been lots of boys and girls in the pool. When Borge asked if there had been more boys than girls swimming, the boy hesitated and then replied: "I don't know. They didn't have clothes on."

22

Farewell, My Unlovely

At noon today I said goodbye to New York forever, thus joining that growing group of people who, for one reason or another, has decided the city is no longer to their liking. That timeless subject — the death of the city of New York — continues to be disinterred with appropriate sounds of anger and anguish by those of us who should know better. When you examine the reality closely, though, you quickly realize that it is not a dying city, that most of the eight million people who huddle together on this tiny rock live there through choice, and while they are aware there is an undiagnosed ailment in the city's bloodstream, they are willing to stick it out. It must have been fun to live in New York once; perhaps it will again. Those of us who are quitting are the impatient ones, the ones who lack the imagination to believe that the bright dream will ever reappear.

The sad aspect of my departure was that there was so little sadness connected with it, and after ten years it seemed to me that I should have looked back with some slight mistiness in my eyes. Of course, New York and I were never married; we had a dalliance for ten years and never anything more serious. No vows were ever exchanged, no affection expressed. A lot of literature has been written on this subject — the disenchanted New Yorker — and I've read a lot of it but none of the cases seem to fit precisely my feelings about the city. I don't hate New York; there is nothing there really to hate and certainly very little to love. It is a city of indifference, and that's the problem. I found I could only give indifference in return.

Many people find New York an unattractive city to inhabit because of the physical filth and while God knows the city is filthy I doubt that that element plays an important role in their decision to leave. Naples is far dirtier, and so are Bombay and countless other cities, but a tolerance for dirt seems to grow where some fondness exists. Tangiers is one of the dirtiest cities in the world, yet a friend of mine who possesses flawless taste lives in the Casbah there and would live nowhere else. A few days ago in Central Park I saw a man leaning on a litter can drinking a carton of orange juice and when he finished he tossed the container not in the receptacle he was leaning against but on the ground. I don't understand this but there is a lot about New York I don't understand. Mainly, I don't understand why the city has no soul, no detectable heartbeat, why the chief element in the city's emotional economy is indifference. I think that's what sent me on my way. Vienna almost suffocates the Viennese with care, Paris manages to imbue her own with an obsession for their fulfillment, San Francisco exudes a pride that even gathers to her heart total strangers, but the key to New York's character is that it doesn't really care about anything. Across the court from the Manhattan apartment that I occupied for the past few years is a dog that quite often hurls insults into the darkness, a few of which my dog refuses to accept service on and replies tartly. I think I yearn for the people of New York to do somewhat the same thing; I would like to think they possess a nature that could be stimulated by something.

A number of New Yorkers have been driven from the city by fear, by the feeling that they are besieged and that if they venture too far from their neighborhood they will be mugged or, worse, murdered. I have never been mugged or physically molested in any way, possibly because my size does not make me an ideal prospect for a hoodlum. Yet I recall the lady who was buying a magazine in the Port Authority Bus Terminal one evening and a stranger walked up and disemboweled her with a butcher knife. Later arrested, he told police that he didn't know the lady but "just felt like killing somebody." It's impossible to protect oneself from such madness, and I think it is the fool in New York who is not a coward at heart. I recall, too, the New Year's Eve when after a dinner party a friend of mine went down to the street to get a taxicab, and the cab veered too quickly and hit him. His wife and I carried him in the cab quickly to Lenox Hill Hospital, and while we were trying to get him emergency treatment, the cabdriver was screaming at us for his fare from the point of the accident to the hospital. A few weeks ago a fifteen-year-old girl was raped on a subway train, and the next day the police announced that the girl was partially responsible for the act because she had entered a car in which there were no other passengers. All of these things may happen in other large cities, and undoubtedly do, but they reflect a lack of caring, a sickness of the soul, that I find difficult to accept and impossible to forget.

Crime is widespread and New York's crime statistics are

not the worst in the country. Perhaps what troubles me are the kinds of crimes that go on here, the terrible meanness on top of the offense. I have just read in the paper that three elderly people, all confined to wheelchairs because of cerebral palsy, were robbed by intruders. Three Mexican visitors, who could speak no English, were charged $167 for a taxi ride from Kennedy International Airport to downtown New York. The 217 blind newsdealers of New York recently complained that their customers are stealing coins from their trays, shortchanging them, and frequently they are mugged by the same individuals on their way home at night. A guard at a savings bank who assisted blind customers with their deposit and withdrawal slips was recently charged with forgery and grand larceny after a blind depositor discovered her balance was $169 instead of the $2,857 which her Braille accounting indicated was due. During last year's Central Park Bicycle Race, five of the racers were attacked and had their bikes stolen while the race was in progress. This is something of a handicap in a bicycle race.

I can offer no ready acceptance of the theory that New York's staggering size creates meanness in the same proportion. The girls in the shadows of the Madeleine in Paris whisper a soft *"Bon soir"* to their prospective customers, but those in New York seem to feel a need for offensive weapons, as the former finance minister of West Germany discovered when he was accosted by two prostitutes in front of the Plaza Hotel and robbed of $180.

And there is the minor cheating too, so commonplace that it is almost a game with New Yorkers. They run through traffic lights for five or six seconds after the light has turned red, and it stirs them with pleasure. The cabdriver conveniently neglects to throw his flag upon arrival at your destination, and while you are paying him, an additional ten cents rings up. It pleases him more than any other money he made all day. The hatcheck girl has no change for a dollar. Almost everybody in New York cheats a little.

I had not intended to dwell excessively upon crime in New York and I have offered these examples more to show the nature of the crimes than their extent. Nor am I vastly concerned about the politics of the city, since the political structure is almost totally controlled by the labor unions, and the options left open to the mayor and the city council are so slight as to make them both ceremonial institutions and little more. Russell Baker, whose satire very often brings him close to the hot fire of truth, once wrote that he was quite familiar with the New York phenomenon called "Strike of the Week," in which the unions take turns at stopping some vital service, but he marveled not that these strikes occur but that New Yorkers accept the inconveniences so passively. It is true, of course. The indifference that I can't seem to keep from returning to has often led me to wonder if a point anywhere exists where New Yorkers will say, "Enough. I will tolerate this no longer." I don't think so. During the famous blackout ten years ago, a woman sat in a stalled subway train for eight hours with a fresh bakery cake in her lap. When asked why she hadn't eaten the cake, she replied: "I just didn't care that much." That's real indifference.

I don't want to see children in Central Park playing in unmarked clumps of poison ivy, and I don't want to see any more statues and walls scribbled with spray paint, and I don't want to ride anymore on an obsolete and rundown subway system so poorly marked that even the Transit Authority people find it difficult to give directions. For some reason, I resent the horrid smartness of a city that sends hundreds of people to eat at Elaine's, a celebrity-packed restaurant serving mediocre food, because it's fashionable to be seen there.

New York offers some prizes I shall miss, and I can only hope to find them elsewhere. A few days ago, after a quick rainstorm, I walked across Central Park near the lake and I thought I had never seen a city so lovely. The steel and glass buildings caught the sunlight, and in the clean air they glowed brilliantly. I passed a kid on Seventy-fourth Street one morning recently and for no reason at all he smiled and said, "Hi." In no city in the whole world are there such beautiful girls; they stride rapidly and with purpose, their faces are filled with vitality, and they seem to meet life eagerly. The tempo of the city itself is exhilarating.

And so I come to the bottom line. I really don't think I want to live in a city where a woman advertises for a lost dog and receives dozens of telephone calls from a variety of people saying they are torturing the animal and will continue to unless she pays large sums of money, or in a city where I am told I must always have $10 in my wallet for a possible mugger because without that I will surely be stabbed, or in a city where my mailman leaves a slip in my box at Christmas suggesting the size of the tip he expects. I shall find some of these things wherever I go, and perhaps all of them, but I don't think so. But above all I want to get away from the indifference of New York. I want to care and — it sounds implausibly poignant — be cared about. So I am leaving New York, but not without some regret. The regret, of course, is mine. New York doesn't give a damn. It has seen thousands of us come and go.

23

Islands

MORE and more people are seeking out islands, I read in the newspaper recently, in the hope of finding freedom from neighborhood blight, crime, atmospheric pollution, noise, and the general fears and insecurity of a troubled world. The law of supply and demand having asserted itself, the article continued, habitable islands are becoming almost impossible to acquire.

I live during the more moderate months of the year on a small island close to the coast of Maine, and perhaps I can furnish a footnote on the prizes — and shortcomings — of island life. There are some general fears and insecurity on islands too, and the fact that they involve nature rather than the mischief of man makes them no less real.

At high tide, the island on which I dwell contains about three and a half acres; it is heavily wooded in oak, spruce, and birch, and like all land on this strange and beautiful coast it offers only a rocky shoreline to the sea. There is only one house on the island, and one walks down a short path from the dwelling to a small, one-room cottage which, in its more important days, served as a handyman's lodging, and later as a toolhouse. Now it has declined further in purpose, and functions only as a writer's workroom.

On the ridiculously small porch of this building, I am writing these lines. My boxer, as is her habit, followed me down the path this morning, and while I wheeled the type-writer table out so I could work in the sun, she struck out on her daily exploratory ramble of the island. She is very curious about what the tides leave on the rocks, and from time to time she brings some extraordinary prize to the door of my study and lays it solemnly there for my approval. She just brought the skeleton and head of a rotten fish, the sort of thing that may have been tossed from a lobster boat, although lobstermen are frugal people and throw very little away, especially a rotten fish, which is about the best bait there is. At least twice a day she noisily invades a rock ledge at one end of the island, scattering the gulls resting there and causing a commotion that doesn't die down for an hour or more. I think of the rock ledge as the Golan Heights of the island; I doubt that I shall ever see lasting peace there.

I believe that the man who lives on an island builds his isolation without meaning to and sooner or later it begins to take possession of his soul. But it brings him a serenity and sureness, a trust in himself that he may never have known before, and he is better for it. Whether he desires it or not, he finds himself the center of his world, the arbiter between man and nature, the monarch of a miniature kingdom, the keeper of peace and the protector of lives, and the occasional intermediary in dealing with a higher power — with fretful winds and fickle seas and lightning and drought. He must be a caretaker, a carpenter, a painter, a physician, a veterinarian; on one occasion which shall always remain

green in my memory, I was called upon to lend an under-
standing ear to a confession of wrongdoing.

Most island dwellers I have known are innately humble
people; I have never heard one say to a visitor, "This is the
greatest place in the world." I'm sure the words have been
spoken, but I think rarely, and never in my presence. If
you like the island, the owner is pleased; if you do not, he is
not offended nor does he appear to be troubled in the least.
No one knows better than he how incomplete and imper-
fect things are, how much needs to be done.

Perhaps one of the gravest errors people make is the
assumption that island life is a simple life. Quite the contrary, it is immensely complicated, with every effort intri-
cately dovetailed with another in the hope of satisfying the
ultimate ambition, which is the avoidance of an unnecessary trip to the mainland. Although this island is quite close
to the Maine coast — I can row the distance in ten minutes
and on one occasion I even swam ashore — I find myself
planning with all the seriousness of a military campaign
how to manage one more day without bridging that gap
between island and mainland. Of course, food and mail
must be brought over regularly, although where the latter
is concerned the dog demurs; this is a presumption, she
thinks, not supported by the facts, and sometimes I agree.

Trips to the mainland are not casual: lists are taken,
logistics are studied (the liquor store and the paint store are
conveniently close together; the post office, on the other
hand, is some distance away and is visited only when
stamps are urgently needed), the tide chart is consulted
(lugging heavy packages up the ramp at low tide clearly
reflects poor planning), and thought is given to the arrival
time of the rural delivery mailman at our mailbox. There

are lesser considerations, such as making telephone calls when the recipient of the call may likely be at home (remember, there are no telephones on small islands), but these must find their place in the overall pattern of the expedition and they cannot expect to exert much influence on the master plan.

Weather is an extremely personal thing to island dwellers, and occupies their thoughts in a way that mainland people would find difficult to understand. Walking out of the house, one makes contact with the elements, whether good or bad, pleasant or unpleasant. In rain, there is no taxicab or automobile to run to, but rather a wet boat that is likely to get wetter still before it reaches land. I never cease to be amazed at how quickly rainwater collects in the bottom of a boat. But one is close, too, to the bright days, to the mottled sunlight shining between the young leaves of the oak trees in the spring, and to the short, golden days of autumn when the shadows begin to slant and the water sparkles in a way that is almost blinding.

Fogs are frequent in these waters, and they don't creep in on tiny cat feet as Carl Sandburg imagined; they move in solidly and with a great show of authority and they often stick around long after their welcome has worn thin. But there is something quite pleasant about the sound of the foghorns in the channel and about that gray, opaque cloud that advances like a wall and wraps the trees and the ledges and the dock in a ghostly shroud. I have been in a rowboat when the fog came in so thickly that I could not see the tips of the oars, and then it was not so pleasant, but later, walking toward the house and seeing the yellow glow of the oil lamps and candles through the windows, I was struck by the cheer and warmth and snugness that shone through the mist. Yes, the weather fits closely to the island dweller, almost like the clothes that he wears, and the first thing he does upon awakening is to glance at the shadows on the wall to see what is likely to be in store for the day.

Of course, sophistication and smartness have come to many islands, especially those used as weekend refuges of the wealthy. Generators supply electricity, there is color television, and one finds music at the swimming pool as well as floodlit tennis courts. I think of these places as extensions of the mainland, as spiritual peninsulas rather than islands, because the concept of insularity has not gripped the hearts and minds of the owners. I have often considered the installation of a generator here, but I have always discarded the notion because I can't bear the thought of an internal combustion engine shattering the silence that envelops this place. Total silence is nothing at all; it is no prize in itself, but it provides an acoustical background against which the sounds of nature are reflected clear and true — of water lapping in the darkness against the dock, of wind whispering through the spruce trees, of a gull squawking disdainfully as it buzzes the house at midnight. I would hate to have these sounds drowned out by an engine.

Thoughts of secession, however mad, nibble like mischievous mice at the mind of the true islander; he knows it can never happen but he derives great satisfaction from contemplating it. I once went through a period — we were all young once — of referring to the mainland as the United States, and I thought of my shopping expeditions there as trips to a foreign country. (My foreign policy, at the time, extended to the United States a most-favored-nation status, and I was not above receiving foreign aid of a nonmilitary nature.) This only illustrates how deeply the fantasy of sovereignty resides in the islander's heart and how stubbornly the wistful dream of self-sufficiency occupies his thoughts.

I must be fair and acknowledge that the threat of loneliness is a constant condition of island life; a small concern to some and a terror to others. But loneliness is not unknown on the mainland, and unless an island is very remote and far at sea one can always go ashore to a movie or to a tavern or to whatever one's heart draws one to that will fill the emptiness.

For some reason that I cannot explain there is an *intensity* to life on an island; beauty is exaggerated, is felt more deeply. A few days ago I put on foul-weather gear and went down on the rocks to welcome a late summer thunderstorm. It was tremendously exciting to stand on the windward side and watch the sky darkening to a dull gray, and to feel the rush of warm, wet air that precedes the arrival of rain. The wind rose quickly, whipping up small whitecaps in the cove, and scattered drops began to fall. They were big and they shook the leaves of the trees violently and left large spots on the rocks, but in a few moments the patter had become a wall of rain, which beat against the rock on which I stood and which searched out, successfully, a dozen cracks in my oilskins. Gusts now tugged at the trees and the bayberries behind me and built great troughs in the sea. Lightning flashed wickedly, followed by instantaneous thunder that rolled across the sky, booming and echoing until it faded away. But soon the strength of the storm weakened, and the thunder moved further and further into the distance. The clouds still hung low and scudded across the sea, but all violence was spent and a gentle rain remained. In a little while I could see light in the western sky, and a shaft of sunlight appeared, bathing the island in a weird, yellow-green light. The summer storm was over.

On an island the corrosion of progress is as great as the owner will tolerate, and no greater. That fragment of land, floating in the sea, offers the rare opportunity of creating a world of one's own, and the blame for failure is pinpointed with terrible accuracy. In 1835, a hardheaded New Englander looked at the villages and cities around him and wrote in his journal: "It does look sometimes as if the world were on its last legs." If Henry David Thoreau were roaming the countryside today, I think one would find him on an island. And on one as far as possible from the smell of industrial smoke, gasoline, and pizza.